BASIC

 HOLDEN-DAY · San Francisco

 **HOLDEN-DAY**   San Francisco

Düsseldorf   •   Johannesburg   •   London
Panama   •   Singapore   •   Sidney

BASIC

A COMPUTER PROGRAMMING LANGUAGE
WITH BUSINESS AND MANAGEMENT APPLICATIONS
Third Edition

C. CARL PEGELS
State University of New York • Buffalo

ROBERT C. VERKLER
California State University • Los Angeles

Holden-Day *Computer and Information Sciences Series*

Coleman and Riley: MIS: MANAGEMENT DIMENSIONS
Kossack and Henschke: INTRODUCTION TO STATISTICS AND
    COMPUTER PROGRAMMING
Makridakis and Wheelwright: INTERACTIVE FORECASTING
Maurer: PROGRAMMING: AN INTRODUCTION TO COMPUTER
    TECHNIQUES
Pavlovich and Tahan: COMPUTER PROGRAMMING IN *BASIC*
Pegels and Verkler: *BASIC*: A COMPUTER PROGRAMMING LANGUAGE
    WITH BUSINESS AND MANAGEMENT APPLICATIONS, Revised Ed.
Reilly and Federighi: THE ELEMENTS OF DIGITAL COMPUTER
    PROGRAMMING
Rosenberg: INTRODUCTION TO *IBM/360* ASSEMBLER LANGUAGE
Sass: *FORTRAN IV,* PROGRAMMING AND APPLICATIONS
Weingarten: TRANSLATION OF COMPUTER LANGUAGES

BASIC
A Computer Programming Language

Copyright © 1978 by Holden-Day, Inc.
500 Sansome Street, San Francisco, California 94111

Library of Congress Catalog Card Number: 78-61168
ISBN: 0-8162-6684-0

Printed in the United States of America

234567890   8079

PREFACE

This third edition of *BASIC: A Computer Programming Language* intends to provide the reader with important additional tools for using BASIC in the business environment. The primary objective of the highly successful prior edition has been retained: to get the readers quickly acquainted with computers and what they can do to solve business problems.

BASIC, as a programming language, has the special capability to do this and has been widely accepted as the standard method for timesharing. This edition intends to summarize the rather simple methods and statements that have made BASIC so popular. In addition, an attempt has been made to introduce some of the newer techniques which have been developed more recently for specialized business applications. The text, for example, has borrowed from such business versions as BASIC-PLUS, BUSINESS BASIC, and modifications of EXBASIC.

The text is unique in many other respects. Much of the scope and content of the subject material resulted from a major computer application — the SOCRATES© System developed by the Chancellor's Office, California State University & Colleges. Surveys were made of the faculty to better organize the material and to provide suitable questions for the BASIC portion of the large data bank.

As a result, some features have been added, not often included in an introductory text, such as:

1. A brief discussion of Batch BASIC, at times useful in processing data for business.
2. A more detailed discussion of character string manipulation, also very useful for business.
3. An in-depth coverage of File Processing for storing and manipulating data and programs.
4. A wide variety of business application problems — from Accounting to Production.

5. An introduction to the use of BASIC for microcomputers.
6. An Instructor's Guide that will be especially useful for computer-oriented faculty. The guide will have supplements available for a particular system — an initial one being the PDP-11 (Digital Equipment Corp.). For those with access to SOCRATES, sample test questions are presented which will be retrievable from the system.

We are especially grateful to those who have been helpful in activities related to the development of the final manuscript. Specifically we want to thank Allen Button, Digital Equipment Corp., Ken Cureton, Chancellor's Office (CSUC), and the faculty, California State University, Los Angeles,* for assistance on technical details.

C. Carl Pegels
R. C. Verkler

---

*Profs. J. Gessford, C. Craft, S. Hartman, R. Lemos, J. Hatch, D. DeBeau, and others.

CONTENTS

1 INTRODUCTION TO COMPUTER PROGRAMMING   **1**

The Computer and the Computer Program
Modes of Operation—Timesharing
Modes of Operation—Batch Processing

2 PROGRAM PREPARATION   **7**

Testing the Finished Program
Flowcharting—An Aid to Advanced BASIC
System and Program Flowcharts
Using the Flowchart
Alternate Flowcharting Methods
Decision Tables

3 FUNDAMENTALS OF PROGRAMMING IN BASIC   **13**

Structure of a BASIC Program
BASIC Statements and Their Elements
    Executable and Nonexecutable Statements
    Line Numbers
    Keywords
    Variables
    Expressions
    Numbers (Constants)
    Mathematical Operators
    E Notation

4 ELEMENTARY OPERATIONS   **21**

Assignment Statement—LET
BASIC Input and Output Statements
    The READ and DATA Statement

The PRINT Statement
Output Control Format
The TAB Functional Operator
The PRINT USING Statement
The INPUT Statement
Special Statements
REM and COMMENT for Documentation
The END Statement

5 BRANCHING AND LOOPING   35
Branching or Transfer Statements
The GO TO Statement
The STOP Statement
The ON-GO TO Statement
The Computed GO TO Statement
The IF-THEN Statement
Relational Symbols
Using the IF Statement
Looping Statements
The FOR-NEXT Statement
Summary

6 ARITHMETIC OPERATIONS   51
Algebraic Operations and General Rules
Mathematical Functions
SQR Function
INT Function
DEF Function

7 SYSTEM COMMANDS   59
Typical System Commands
RUN
NEW
LIST
SAVE, OLD, and UNSAVE
CATALOG or CAT
DELETE
RENUMBER or REN
To Alter a Program in Storage
RENAME
Commands to Terminate

8 SUBSCRIPTS AND ARRAYS   **67**
   Subscripted Variables
      Subscript as a Variable
      Subscripts as Accumulators
   The DIM Statement
   Arrays
      Reverse-Order Arrays
      Sorting with Arrays
      Two-Dimensional Arrays

9 MATRIX OPERATIONS   **75**
   The Matrix Operators
   Matrix without the DIM
   Special Features of Matrix Commands
   MAT INPUT Statement
   Vector Statements

10 CHARACTER STRINGS   **87**
   String Constants
   String Variables
   Special Character-String Uses
      Strings with Matrices
      Relational Operators
      ASCII Conversions
      String Input
      String Functions

**11 SUBROUTINES AND SPECIAL
    FEATURES**   **95**
   GOSUB Statement
   Special Features
      Replacing Variables or Constants with an Expression

12 PROGRAMMING WITH DATA FILES   **105**
   Common File-Handling Statements
   File Preparation
   Using Files in a Program
   File Designator
   Special Features of Files
   Advanced File Approaches
      The OPEN Statement

The CLOSE Statement
The KILL Statement
The CHAIN Statement
GET and PUT

13 A SELECTION OF BUSINESS AND   119
    ECONOMICS PROBLEMS
    Payroll Preparation
    Depreciation Calculation
    Average- and Marginal-Cost Calculations
    Breakeven Analysis
    Compound-Interest Calculation

14 PRODUCTION-MANAGEMENT   131
    PROBLEMS
    Order Point and Order Quantity
    Ratio Scheduling
    Learning-Curve Calculation

15 RANDOM NUMBERS AND SIMULATION   141
    Random-Number Generation
    The RANDOMIZE Statement
    Simulation of Simple Processes
    Junior Merchant's Problem Simulation
    A Queuing Simulation

16 CORPORATE FINANCIAL MODELS   151
    What Is a Financial Model?
    Development of the Model
    Conclusion

17 A SELECTION OF STATISTICS   161
    PROBLEMS
    Sum of a Series
    Calculating Averages (Means)
    Calculating the Geometric Mean
    Calculating the Median
    Deviations
    Determining Deviations
    Expected-Value Calculations
    Binomial Probabilities
    Poisson Probabilities
    Bayesian Probabilities

Fibonacci Numbers
Goodness-of-Fit Test

18 MICROCOMPUTERS AND BASIC   181
Programming a Microcomputer
Use of System Commands
Statements
Strings and Concatenation
Functions
File Manipulation
Chaining
Array Limits

APPENDICES
Appendix A: Vectors and Matrices   187
Appendix B: BASIC and Its Business Derivatives   197
Appendix C: Additional BASIC Features Available   203
              for Some Systems
Appendix D: Batch BASIC Summary and References   207
Appendix E: Commands and Statements of   209
              Four Selected Microcomputer
              Systems
Appendix F: Solutions to Selected Exercises   211

1 INTRODUCTION TO COMPUTER PROGRAMMING

A computer program is a written message between the computer programmer and the computer. The message is written in a computer programming language. BASIC is the name of the computer programming language used in this book. There are also other useful computer languages such as FORTRAN, COBOL, and RPG. However, we shall restrict ourselves to the BASIC language only.

Before discussing the BASIC language in detail, you must first become familiar with the steps involved in developing and using a computer program. They are:

1. Writing a computer program for performing the operations required to solve a problem or to process data.
2. Sending the program to the computer (also called central processing unit or CPU) by typewriter terminal or other means.
3. Testing and correcting the program if there are errors.
4. Having the program executed by the computer.

Our main concern in this book is with writing the program. If this task is done properly, little correcting will be necessary and the other steps will follow smoothly.

THE COMPUTER AND THE COMPUTER PROGRAM

The typical commercial computer is a complex data processor which can perform a variety of rather routine chores at extremely high speeds. It can perform the simplest of arithmetic operations such as adding and substracting; it has a memory for items it is instructed to memorize; and it can perform simple comparisons, useful in decision-making. It also can store instructions in the form of a computer program.

1

The computer program you write is a set of instructions that tells the computer exactly what to do. The instructions you provide are carried out by the computer in the sequence specified by the program. Another way to describe a computer program is to view it as a recipe. It usually starts with the given data as ingredients, contains a set of operations to be performed on the data in specified order, and finishes with a set of required answers as the end product. If the recipe contains errors, then the end product may be a disaster; and so will a computer program with errors.

A program may also be considered a message in computer language, informing the computer what to do. The message is written in short "sentences" and transferred to the computer by means of a typewriter terminal or similar device. In a timesharing mode, Figure 1-1 portrays the steps the message takes when you, the programmer, forward it by terminal.

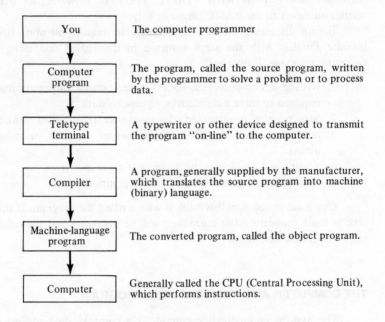

You	The computer programmer
Computer program	The program, called the source program, written by the programmer to solve a problem or to process data.
Teletype terminal	A typewriter or other device designed to transmit the program "on-line" to the computer.
Compiler	A program, generally supplied by the manufacturer, which translates the source program into machine (binary) language.
Machine-language program	The converted program, called the object program.
Computer	Generally called the CPU (Central Processing Unit), which performs instructions.

Figure 1-1
Process Chart of a Computer Program

MODES OF OPERATION—TIMESHARING

A digital computer provides results in two ways— the timesharing mode and the batch processing mode. Each mode has its advantages depending on the type of business application. The BASIC language is considered a timesharing-type language—so we will discuss this method first.

Timesharing is a literal description. Several users in different locations share the same computer, which usually is at a place far removed from the users. At any time each of several users, working from a terminal such as the Teletype Corporation Model 33 or the Digital Equipment Corporation's newer RSTS-11, has the illusion that he or she is the only user. Actually, many users are possible due to the control of scheduling. The computer processes a part of each user's problem in turn. Each user uses the terminal to type and transmit instructions (programs and data) to the computer, and the computer response is printed out by the terminal typewriter. Mistakes in the program are detected (and can usually be corrected) immediately.

To make contact with the computer, the user turns on the terminal, picks up a telephone (usually attached to the typewriter terminal), and dials the computer. When a connection is made, you will hear a high-pitched tone. The telephone should now be returned to the cradle. The computer starts the conversation by generally typing out some messages (usually requests). To better follow this man-machine interaction, the series of events shown in Example 1 are an illustration of a typical terminal printout. The procedure is slightly different if an acoustic coupler is used to connect the teletypewriter terminal with an ordinary telephone.

From the sample printout and the indicated dialog one can make some generalizations for most timesharing operations. The steps include:

1. User turns on typewriter terminal and dials computer telephone number.
2. When hookup is made, computer sends message signaling successful connection.
3. User provides identification and supplies information such as whether a new or old program will be used, the programming language, etc.
4. User, if writing a program, types BASIC program statements.
5. At end of program, user types RUN or other similar execute command. If executable, results are typed by the typewriter according to instructions. If in error, the program is not executed, and diagnostic error messages are printed out instead. These errors can be corrected, and immediately another attempt can be made.
6. Program and results can be listed (printed out in entirety or partially). If not saved, it is immediately released.

Example 1

Turn terminal ON

Typewriter printout (not given)		
HELLO	(CR)	User command to request service
System banner appears #project number, programmer number	(CR)	Identification
PASSWORD; password	(CR)	Computer asks for valid password—does not print
Message of the day		System messages appear optionally
READY		
OLD CHCKBK	(CR)	Name of the new program to be run
READY		
LIST	(CR)	Allows printed listing of program at terminal
CHCKBK 15:24 1–FEB–76		
110 REM BALANCING CHECKBOOK	(CR)	
120 REM B=OLD BALANCE	(CR)	
130 REM C=CHANGE IN BALANCE	(CR)	
140 REM N=NEW BALANCE	(CR)	A program to balance a checkbook
150 LET B=1.99	(CR)	
160 LET N=B	(CR)	
170 READ C	(CR)	
180 IF C=0 THEN 210	(CR)	
190 LET N=N+C	(CR)	
200 GO TO 170	(CR)	
210 PRINT "NEW BALANCE IS $",N	(CR)	
220 DATA 1000,–250,–150.99, –600,200,0	(CR)	User input of data
230 END	(CR)	
READY		
RUN	(CR)	Allows user to begin execution of program in core, or one or more lines of answer; computer prints answer
CHCKBK 15.25 1–FEB–76		
NEW BALANCE IS $ 201.00		
READY		
BYEF	(CR)	Start of logout procedure; indicates wish to leave terminal

Turn terminal OFF

The program portion of Example 1 will be more understandable after Chapter 3 is completed. Essentially, it computes a current balance in a checking account. Programming details will be explained in subsequent chapters—when we begin to put the BASIC language to work. At this time it is more important to convince you that simple programs can be developed quite easily through a computer—and errors are not all that serious because most can be corrected as they occur.

MODES OF OPERATION—BATCH PROCESSING

In batch processing, a number of jobs are read into the computer and processed sequentially. A job refers to a program and the sets of input data to be processed—usually by a punched card system. Large quantities of data can be read into the computer with this method, but there may be considerable delays in processing. After the processing is finished, the results are normally printed in reports.

Batch BASIC requires, in some cases, some different symbols because it is dependent often on the type of input device—whether keypunch or keytape system. For keypunch systems such as IBM 029, we must use, for example, the ** for ↑ and the single apostrophe for the double quote. These differences are noted in Appendix D.

This purposely brief discussion of batch BASIC is intended to have the user recognize that such a capability does exist on some systems. The authors have processed the programs in this text in batch on the CDC 3150 and 3300. Although the approach is limited in comparison to such languages as COBOL, it should be considered for certain business applications. Chapter 12, Programming with Data Files, can be utilized for possible approaches to the need for manipulating files in batch BASIC.

CONCLUSIONS

With computer timesharing and batch processing, even the smallest business or educational institution can afford the luxury, convenience, and prestige of computer accessibility. Costs of computer hardware capable of handling BASIC are steadily decreasing as the result of technological improvements and miniaturization. Mini-computers, and even microprocessors, can utilize BASIC because of its relative simplicity. The BASIC language presented in this book provides a quick guide for any potential user.

EXERCISES

1. What can a computer do over and above what a mechanical desk calculator can do?

2. Why would the computer request a user number?

3. Diagram the flow of information in any firm or organization with which you are familiar. Determine what kinds of information are important, and then consider how a terminal could be of help in this process.

4. What is wrong with using the terminal for processing large amounts of data? What system may be superior, and how would you handle such large amounts of data?

5. The chapter related how a terminal exercise was conducted. Why must a programmer be familiar with details of a process such as this?

6. Name some typical business applications that timesharing would be especially good for. Do the same for batch processing.

7. Write a series of short steps you would use to secure an old file named SALES from a typical timesharing system.

2 PROGRAM PREPARATION

Preparing a computer program in BASIC, or in any other language, takes two steps. They are:

1. Analyzing, studying, and defining the problem and developing a plan or program to solve the problem.
2. Writing the program in the computer language, BASIC in this case. This step is called coding the program.

The first step may also involve the use of a flowchart if the problem is complex. The second step is relatively easy if the programmer knows the language and if step one has been performed satisfactorily.

TESTING THE FINISHED PROGRAM

Ideally, a program runs correctly as written; but unfortunately, this is not the normal case. Simple mistakes occur in typing or keypunch—and are then rather easily identified and corrected. Typing and syntactical errors are noted as the program is typed at the keyboard. Appropriate error messages notify the programmer, giving him the opportunity to "debug" his program immediately. More complex logical errors are not quickly detected, but even here the computer provides an effective method to evaluate the entire program as a unit for common errors.

The test-and-debug process continues until the results are satisfactory. The fact that a program can be executed (no critical errors) does not mean that it is well written from an efficiency standpoint. Some will find the process of programming an interesting and rather easy task. Others will need considerable help to build error-free and efficient programs. It is the purpose of this book to teach you how to become a proficient programmer through the developing and writing of numerous programs.

7

FLOWCHARTING—AN AID TO ADVANCED BASIC

Most computer programs are difficult to visualize without some sort of diagram. The most popular diagram aid is called the flowchart. Its preliminary purpose is to illustrate the logic needed to solve a problem. It also is of considerable help when the program must be modified by someone other than the original programmer, and as a memory guide for the original programmer if he returns to the program at a later time. Errors in logic are most easily corrected through the flowchart, since it clearly demonstrates the interconnections among all parts of the program.

SYSTEM AND PROGRAM FLOWCHARTS

Two general types of flowcharts are used in data processing operations. A system flowchart depicts the broad objectives and what must be accomplished by an organization and its personnel. Emphasis would be on paper flow and work stations, requiring many symbols representing documents and operations.

What we will use in conjunction with the coding introduced in this text is the program flowchart. This type depicts computer decisions and processes. Relatively few symbols are needed to do this task. (See Figure 2-1.)

USING THE FLOWCHART

Figure 2-2 illustrates the relationship of the flowchart to the requirements of the program. In doing a program, it is often more systematic to keep in mind what the inputs are to be, and what is to be the format of the report to be outputted by the program. To expand this form, we could include on the right side all the appropriate BASIC coding corresponding to each block on the chart. One helpful device would be to include line numbers, or segment numbers, on or next to the different symbol depictions.

ALTERNATE FLOWCHARTING METHODS

The new HIPO method (Hierarchy plus Input-Process-Output) developed by IBM is a more active solution to the problem of improving programming documentation. In this method the symbols

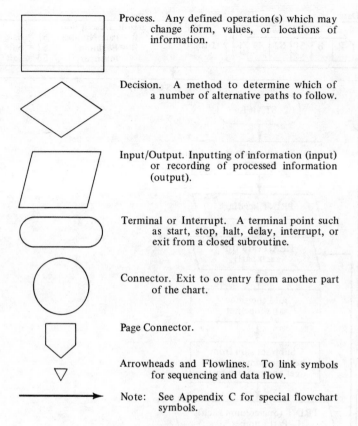

Process. Any defined operation(s) which may change form, values, or locations of information.

Decision. A method to determine which of a number of alternative paths to follow.

Input/Output. Inputting of information (input) or recording of processed information (output).

Terminal or Interrupt. A terminal point such as start, stop, halt, delay, interrupt, or exit from a closed subroutine.

Connector. Exit to or entry from another part of the chart.

Page Connector.

Arrowheads and Flowlines. To link symbols for sequencing and data flow.

Note: See Appendix C for special flowchart symbols.

Figure 2-1
BASIC Flowcharting Symbols

are designed to segment the program into blocks and then build the hierarchy of a given function with the blocks. The special template for this method is illustrated in Appendix C. In some extremely complex problem analyses, it may be necessary to set up a series of connecting tables, to utilize detailed block diagrams which will record actual coding, or to use symbols more special than those approved by the American National Standards Institute.

DECISION TABLES

An alternate form of logical display is the "decision table." Often easier to draw than a flowchart, such a table can be more compact and

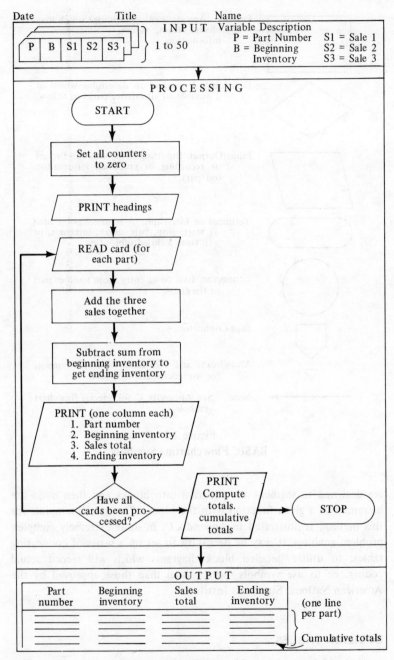

Figure 2-2

Form courtesy of Prof. Clifford Craft, Cal. State Univ.-Los Angeles

Program courtesy of Prof. Edwin Bartenstein, Cal. State Univ.-Northridge.

have excellent summary qualities. A typical table would show the different tests made, the test conditions, and the actions required. Many forms and degrees of sophistication are displayed in these tables. However, Figure 2-3 illustrates one of the more simple outlines.

		Test conditions								
		1	2	3	4	5	6	7	8	9
Tests made	1. Product A	Y	Y	N	N	N	N	N	N	
	2. Product B	N	Y	N	Y	Y	N	N	Y	
Actions	1. Go 9-Test			x			x	x		
	2. Go 10-Test		x							

Figure 2-3

EXERCISES

1. Give at least two reasons for preparing flowcharts.

2. What flowcharting symbols would you use for the following BASIC actions?
    a. Reading in data values
    b. Making a comparison
    c. Printing a new report
    d. Stopping the program

3. Draw a flowchart for computing the weekly pay for several employees. The data that should be read in for each employee are the employee's name, base pay, and number of hours worked. The flowchart should compute, for each employee, the regular 40-hour gross pay, overtime at time and a half, and total gross pay. The output should be name and base pay rate, total hours worked, regular gross pay, overtime gross pay, and total gross pay.

4. Prepare a decision table that inputs and outputs four values, finds the largest of those values, and then outputs this largest value.

3 FUNDAMENTALS OF PROGRAMMING IN BASIC

BASIC is a relatively simple and useful programming language because a small number of statement types perform solutions to almost any problem. The development of the BASIC language was supported by the National Science Foundation under the direction of Professors John G. Kemeny and Thomas E. Kurtz. Since its development, BASIC has been adopted by many commercial computer timesharing systems. This is primarily because of its conversational nature. A "conversational" language is one which allows the user to communicate directly with the processor and receive responses as part of a man/machine relationship.

BASIC is also becoming more widely available as a language for in-house computers with batch and timesharing capability. The BASIC language is a mixture of simple English and mathematics. Anyone able to read this book will, of course, be able to handle the English part. Likewise, the mathematics is mainly elementary arithmetic and algebra. The symbology is explained as it arises.

The alphabet of BASIC consists of:

1. All the normal English alphabetic letters.
2. The numeric symbols 0-9.
3. Special characters, such as +, -, *, /, =, #, @, :, and $.

Other special characters are used as part of the character set of a particular terminal or keypunch machine. They will vary, therefore, with the manufacturer or the model.

In learning BASIC, primary attention should be given to the elementary statements. However, as the student becomes more proficient and as new programming features develop, more complex tasks can be attempted. Program efficiencies are of major importance in any language.

13

STRUCTURE OF A BASIC PROGRAM

Each instruction is written as a separate statement. Thus a complete BASIC program will be composed of a sequence of statements. Such statements must appear in the order in which they will be executed unless a deliberate branch is made. Let us assume you have a simple arithmetic problem which you want to solve by using the computer. You want to calculate the cost of a quart of milk if a gallon costs $1.25. The following program will do this for you.

Example 1

```
10 REM CØST ØF A QUART ØF MILK
20 LET S = 125
30 LET N = 4
40 LET C = S/N
50 PRINT C
60 END
```

Note that there are six statements or sentences in this example. Each statement is typed on a separate line and is identified by a line number. The six statements above constitute a program in the BASIC language. Each statement gives direction to the computer. Note that each statement begins with an English word describing the action. The first statement (line number 10) identifies the program. The keyword REM (for REMARK) informs the computer that the statement is only for identification purposes and is not part of the instructions to follow. The second statement assigns the cost of a gallon jug (125 cents) to the variable S.

The third statement assigns the number of quarts in a gallon to the variable N. In both statements the assigning of numbers or constants (125 and 4) to the variables (S and N) is performed by using the self-explanatory keyword LET. In line 40 the LET statement is again used, this time to instruct the computer to divide 125 by 4 and to assign the result of that division to the variable C. Note the division symbol (/) that is used. No other symbols for division are allowed in BASIC.

Line 50 contains a statement that instructs the computer to print out the value of the numeric variable which it has calculated. The computer will print out the value C and not the symbol "C" itself. The final statement, on line 60, just tells the computer that the end of the program has been reached.

In the ordinary computer program above, you may have observed that everything had to be spelled out in detail for the computer.

Nothing can be left to chance. The computer must even be told when a program has ended—with and END statement.

The numeric variables S, N, and C used in the program are all single letters. To allow for more variety and a greater number of variables, BASIC has been constructed so that you may add one digit to a letter to form a numeric variable, provided the digit follows the letter. For instance, A and B2 are allowable numeric-variable names, but 6C and KL are not allowed.

We may now go back and analyze the language in more detail.

BASIC STATEMENTS AND THEIR ELEMENTS

The purpose of a statement is to inform the computer what to do. Some statements define the arithmetic operations that the computer must execute. Other statements inform the computer which steps must be repeated, when to move to other parts of the program, and when to end. The latter are generally called control statements because they provide direction or control the computer in completing the task specified by the program. Still other statements describe how and when to read in or print out information, specify the amount of storage required, and specify the data for the program.

Rules for Statements

1. Every statement must appear on a separate line.
2. A statement can't exceed one line in length.
3. Each statement must start with a line number (except in the batch mode).
4. Each statement must have a keyword which indicates the operation to be carried out.

Executable and Nonexecutable Statements

Executable statements are typical Input/Output types (such as READ and PRINT), Assignment statements (such as LET), and Control statements (such as IF and STOP). The nonexecutable statements are for specifications, subprograms, and data. Input/Output statements direct the computer in transmitting information between the CPU and the terminals or other devices. Arithmetic computations and assignments are directed by assignment statements. The logical order in which statements are executed is controlled by the control statement. All of these types will be explained in more detail in later chapters.

Line Numbers

When observing the elements in more detail, we note that each program line in the timesharing mode requires a line number. The batch mode requires line numbers for branches or other special purposes. Line numbers (a) indicate the order in which statements are to be evaluated for execution, (b) provide a means to identify pertinent statements in branching and looping, and (c) allow easy changing of a specified line without affecting other program parts.

Rules for Line Numbers

1. Sequence by positive integers from 1 to as high as 99999, depending on the computer.
2. Increment by 5, 10, 100 to allow for later insertion of lines.
3. Make line numbers progressively higher.
4. Line numbers must be unique.

Keywords

Each statement number must be followed by a BASIC keyword (often called directives, commands, etc.). The keyword indicates the type of instruction to be carried out. Keywords are alphabetic and replace the boxes and symbols of the flowchart. Typical keywords are discussed later in the text, and a more complete listing is presented in Appendix B together with the differences in BASIC dialects.

Variables

Another important element encountered in statements is the variable name. A variable is a data item whose value is changeable—in contrast to a constant. Variables can be assigned values by various statements such as LET, INPUT, and READ. Values remain constant until additional statements conflict.

Rules for Variables

1. A numeric variable must be a single letter or a letter followed by single digit.
2. A variable may contain a subscript or string (the latter is discussed in Chapter 10).
3. Values should be set to zero for counters and accumulators to assure they will not be misinterpreted.

The following are examples of variables:

Correct	Incorrect
K=0 (for setting a value or counter to zero)	AA
A1	5A
A(10) or A$	P6Y

Note: It is advisable to put in REMARK or COMMENT statements to explain the particular variables used in a program.

Expressions

An expression is a group of symbols which supply required or optional values and are used in association with the keyword to define in detail the action taken. Expressions may be formed from combinations of numbers, variables, or functions. Operators separate these elements as needed. The following are examples of expressions:

Arithmetic	Logical
10*3	A>B
A7**(B*3)	(C=D)

Numbers (Constants)

Numbers, often called constants because their values remain constant during the program, are used in expressions to provide a positive or negative value. The following are typical:

Legal	Illegal
+2	$\dfrac{15}{2}$
-3.43	$\sqrt{6}$

Rules for Numbers

1. Avoid all commas in a number,
2. If necessary, precede a number with a + sign or – sign.
3. Use an exponent with a number when appropriate. E notation is noted below.
4. Limit the numbers to 8 or 9 digits for most systems.
5. Keep within the magnitude (however, most systems allow up to a 38th power).

Mathematical Operators

The language handles all elementary arithmetic operations. Formulas are evaluated similarly to standard mathematical notation. Most computers use the following operators:

Operator	Example	Explanation
+ (addition)	X + Y	Add Y to X
– (negation or unary minus)	X – Y	Subtract Y from X
* (multiplication)	X * Y	Multiply X by Y
/ (division)	X / Y	Divide X by Y
↑ or ** (exponentiation)	X**Y	X to the Y power

E Notation

Often the computer gives answers in exponential notation. Very large or very small numbers may be written according to their powers of 10. In BASIC, the letter E is used to designate such a representation, in a rigid format:

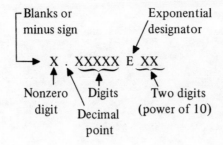

Example 2

   −2.90700E-03 (The value of the number is −2.90700 X 10^{-3} or
   −.00290700.)

EXERCISES

1.   Give an example of an arithmetic statement.

2.   Explain why there are exactly 286 numeric variables (without the
     use of subscripts) in BASIC.

3.   Since E stands for "times ten to the power," can it ever be
     confused with a numeric variable?

4.   What numbers do 5.6E10, .049E5, 46.2E-7, and 16.0E1 stand
     for?

5.   Express as BASIC numbers:
     a.   7,350 (with E also)
     b.   −120
     c. 10^6
     d.   1/6
     e.   .3333333333333
     f.   Four times negative six

6.   Give an example of each:
     a.   A logical expression
     b.   A nonexecutable statement
     c.   A keyword
     d.   A variable
     e.   A constant
     f.   An operator to provide exponentiation on the keypunch

4 ELEMENTARY OPERATIONS

Instructions to perform operations are given in the statements of a program. In this section we discuss the keywords which are part of each statement and which provide information to the computer about what is to be done.

ASSIGNMENT STATEMENT—LET

A common keyword for assignment statements, LET is used for performing certain computations and to set the variable to the left of the equal sign equal to the result. Contrary to algebraic operations and other programming languages, LET is usually spelled out in BASIC. For instance, in Example 1 the following format is used:

Line Number	Keyword	Variable	Operator	Expression
200	LET	A	=	13

Example 1

```
10 LET Y = X2 + X3
15 LET T$ = "HAND"
20 LET Y2 = Y2 + 2
25 LET B = 7.985
30 LET T = S2 = T3 = 4
35 LET K$ = "K"
```

Note that in line 10 the statement contains an ordinary algebraic formula preceded by the word LET. The computer would add X2 and X3 and set Y equal to the sum. Line 20 is nonsense as an algebraic formula but is used extensively in data processing (called a replacement statement). It acts as a counter and increases the value of the variable Y2 by 2 units. Line 30 is also unlike the typical algebraic statement; it

21

assigns the value 4 to three different numeric variables. Lines 15 and 35 contain statements that assign words to string variables (discussed in detail in Chapter 10). Note that a word may consist of only one letter as in line 35. Also note that the letter K in line 35 is different from the numeric variable K used in expressions with numeric variables. In any case, Example 1 shows that a simple keyword such as LET combined with the equal sign can be quite powerful and versatile.

BASIC INPUT AND OUTPUT STATEMENTS

The READ and DATA Statement

The two keywords READ and DATA go together, although they do not appear in the same statement or necessarily follow each other directly. However, for every variable listed after the word READ in a statement, there must follow at some point in the program a statement with the word DATA followed by a constant. The computer matches the first READ variable with the first DATA constant, the second variable with the second constant, etc.

Example 2

```
10 READ A, D, F2
20 DATA 5, −9.24, 12.0065
```

Note in Example 2 that the variables in the READ statement are separated by commas. Similarly, the constants in the DATA statement are separated by commas. Also note that the plus sign is omitted for positive numbers, but for a negative number the minus sign must precede the number.

Example 2 could also have been written as follows:

```
10 READ A, D, F2
20 DATA 5
30 DATA −92.4
40 DATA 12.0065
```

In this form, too, the computer will match the first variable with the first constant, and so on.

The number of DATA statements does not have to equal the number of READ statements, but the number of constants must equal the number of variables appearing in the READ statements. If the number of variables exceeds the number of constants, the computer will print an "out of data" message. If the number of constants exceeds the number of variables, the surplus constants will be ignored.

Since READ statements generally precede DATA statements, the usual practice is to place the READ statements at the beginning of a program and the DATA statements at the end.

Example 3 contains READ and DATA statements with various configurations. Note that the number of variables equals the number of constants.

Example 3

```
100 READ X2, X, Y3, Y2, X4, X5
110 DATA 5, 4.86794, 52, 4.3, −3.4, −49
120 READ A, B, C
130 DATA .64, .0092
140 DATA 576
150 READ A1, B1
160 READ A3, B3, C4
170 DATA 5, 6, 7, 99, 57.64
```

The PRINT Statement

Having discussed the statements which enter data into the computer, we now move to the statement which extracts information from it. This is the PRINT statement, which may also be used to print out a message, or a combination of data and a message. Furthermore, the keyword PRINT by itself will tell the computer to skip a line. Examples of the various functions of the PRINT statement are shown in Example 4.

Example 4

```
120 PRINT A, B, C2, C, D
140 PRINT "YØU MADE A MISTAKE"
180 PRINT "THE ANSWER IS" C2
```

Line 120 contains the PRINT statement which directs the computer to print out the values of the five numeric variables listed. Line 140 directs the computer to print out the message: "YØU MADE A MISTAKE." Note that the double quotation marks enclose the message to be printed out; these quotation marks are not printed out by the computer. In line 180 the PRINT statement directs that a message and the value of the numeric variable C2 be printed out. If the value of C2 were 15, then the computer would cause the typewriter to print out: THE ANSWER IS 15.

In line 120 of Example 4 the variables are separated by commas, but note that commas never follow the keywords in a statement. For instance, LET, READ, DATA, and PRINT are followed immediately by variables or constants or, in the case of string variables, by words. We will return to this later.

A PRINT statement may contain both a message and a variable. If the variable follows the message, then no comma is used (see line 180 of Example 4). However, if a variable precedes a message, then a comma must separate them.

Example 5

```
230 PRINT "THE UNIT" X2, "IS NØT IN STØCK"
235 PRINT
260 PRINT "DATE", "TIME", "PLACE"
265 PRINT D2, T2, P3
```

Line 230 will print out the information that the unit identified by the variable X2 is not in stock. Line 235 just causes the skipping of a line. Line 260 causes three headings to be printed out for the values of the variables in line 265. Thus, if the values of the numeric variables X2, D2, T2, and P3 in Example 5 were, respectively, 59, 1011, 930, and 74, then the printed results of the four statements would appear as follows:

```
THE UNIT 59 IS NØT IN STØCK
DATE    TIME    PLACE
1011     930      74
```

We can now write a practice program utilizing the statements covered above. Suppose you want to calculate the balance and monthly carrying charge on a charge account. You have the option of paying either the entire balance or a minimum payment. If you pay the minimum, you will also have to pay a carrying charge on the difference between the original balance and the minimum payment. If you pay the full balance, there is, of course, no carrying charge. A program that performs the calculations is shown in Example 6. The input variables consist of the numeric variable B which stands for the original balance, the numeric variable P which stands for the minimum payment, and the numeric variable I which stands for the monthly interest rate. The output variables consist of the numeric variable C2 which stands for the difference between the balance and the minimum payment, and the numeric variable C3 which stands for the carrying charge. The reader is urged to analyze the program and printout carefully.

Example 6

```
10 READ B, P, I
20 LET C2 = B —P
30 LET C3 = C2*I/100
40 PRINT "BALANCE LEFT IS $" C2
50 PRINT "CARRYING CHARGE IS $" C3
60 DATA 87.90, 10, 1.5
70 END


RUN


BALANCE LEFT IS $77.90
CARRYING CHARGE IS $1.1685
```

Output Control Format

PRINT statements, in general, are quite straightforward. However, as we saw, the PRINT statement causes the typewriter to skip to a new line each time it appears. As a matter of fact, the PRINT statement can be used by itself to skip a line as shown in Example 5. This is only one use of the PRINT for output control. There are many cases in which better utilization of paper is required or several data items must appear on one line. The most frequently used of these other output controls are:

1. TAB (the output tab function)
2. ; (used to produce a packed format)
3. , (normal item separator)

By typing a comma or semicolon after each variable in the PRINT statement, spacing can be handled to an extent. For instance, the statement

10 PRINT X, Y

will print the values of X and Y on one line, spaced fifteen spaces apart if they are single digits. To keep them closer together, we separate them with the semicolon as in

```
10 PRINT X; Y
```

and they will be printed only two spaces apart if they are single digits.

To put the output of two PRINT statements on one line, we type a comma after the last item of the first statement, as in

```
10 PRINT X, Y,
20 PRINT A, B
```

The values of the four variables shown here will be printed on the same line because of the comma that follows Y. Since there is no comma following B, the typewriter will skip to the next line. To have the four values printed closer together, we could use semicolons; the statement would appear as

```
10 PRINT X; Y;
20 PRINT A; B
```

In computer programming it is frequently desirable to position a certain output at a specific location, but this is not always as easy as in languages such as COBOL and RPG. The following section explains one method to control output this way.

The TAB Functional Operator

The TAB is used as follows: A line is assumed to have 75* columns, numbered from 0 to 74. The function TAB(N) inserted in a PRINT statement will direct the carriage to column N, where N is a numeric (integer) variable to which a value has been previously assigned. Instead of a variable, a constant may be inserted in the parentheses, as in TAB(16). If the carriage has already passed the indicated position, the TAB function is ignored. For instance:

```
10 LET X = 19
20 PRINT P; TAB(X); Q; TAB(32); R
```

will cause P to be printed in column 1, Q in column 19; and R in column 32. Note the use of semicolons in line 20.

TAB functions must be in increasing sequence; otherwise, errors in output occur. For example, PRINT TAB(50); A; TAB(40); B, etc. would give each value beginning at printer position 50 with one or two blanks between numbers. The TAB statement is especially useful for outputting professional accounting and management reports as well as for plotting curves.

---

*Some systems use 72.

The PRINT USING Statement

The PRINT USING statement may also be used in some systems for positioning values on output paper. A constant, variable, or expression can be used in a string which is an exact image of the line to be printed. All characters in the string are printed as they appear in output, except for special formatting characters used in some systems.

Example 7

```
10 DATA 5.025, 2.74, 9.5, .093, 999
20 READ X, Y
30 IF X=999 THEN 70
40 PRINT USING 50, X, Y*
50: #.## #.#
60 GO TO 20
70 END
```

This program will print the values of X and Y, using the values in line 50 as a guide to place digits. The program puts 5.03 and 2.7 at the specified print position as a rounding function in some systems.* The pound (#) sign shows the field width.

Summary of General Output Rules for PRINT

1. Limit the number of significant digits to be printed (depending on the particular system).
2. Suppress leading and trailing zeros. Note that where a number can be represented as an integer, printing of decimal point is suppressed.
3. Extra commas usually cause print zones to be skipped.
4. Most numbers are printed in decimal format unless too large—in which case an E format is used.
5. Normally each output list element is printed in a separate field of the print line, left-justified in the field.
6. It is legal to put a comma after the last list item, which then deletes the carriage return.
7. Double space by using a PRINT statement without a list.
8. Use carriage control characters for special spacing, according to the particular system.

---

*BASIC—PLUS, Digital Equipment Corp. This system combines the PRINT USING with the image (e.g. 40 PRINT USING "#.##" A, B). Note that quotes are required for the string.

The INPUT Statement

The INPUT statement provides the programmer with a tool that can truly make his computer interactive. The person using an interactive program is able to communicate with the computer, in a limited sense: the computer types out certain questions, and the operator responds in the context of his particular problem.

Suppose the data to be used in a program change each time the program is run. The data changes could be accomplished by changing the DATA statement each time, but this would require modification of the program by someone who knows the program. If INPUT statements are used, the computer will indicate exactly when new data are to be entered, and no program changes will be required.

To accomplish this, the programmer incorporates in the computer program, just before the INPUT statement, a PRINT statement instructing the user to type in the required data. The INPUT statement following it will cause the computer to type a question mark at the end of the PRINT statement. This question mark signals the user to type in the requested data. For instance, the subprogram in Example 8 asks the user to type in the age and weight of an individual.

Example 8

```
110 PRINT "TYPE IN THE AGE IN YEARS AND THE"
120 PRINT "WEIGHT IN PØUNDS ØF THE PATIENT";
130 INPUT A1, W1
```

The computer would, of course, work through the preceding parts of the program. It would respond to the subprogram in Example 8 by typing, TYPE IN THE AGE IN YEARS AND THE WEIGHT IN POUNDS OF PATIENT? and waiting for the data. The user would respond by typing in the age and weight, separated by a comma. (If the semicolon had been left off the end of line 120, the question mark would have been printed on the next line.)

INPUT statements should be used only when the data entered do not have to be saved. If data must be saved, they should be made part of a program with READ and DATA statements.

Example 9

```
10 REM THIS PRØGRAM CALCULATES DIVIDEND RATE
15 REM AND PRICE EARNINGS RATIØ ØF A CØMMØN
```

```
20 REM STØCK
25 PRINT "TYPE IN CØRPØRATIØN NAME IN ØNE WØRD";
30 INPUT C$
35 PRINT "TYPE IN CØMMØN STØCK PRICE";
40 INPUT P
45 PRINT "TYPE IN EARNINGS AND DIVIDENT PER SHARE";
50 INPUT E, D
55 LET D2 = D*100/P
60 LET P2 = P/E
65 PRINT "FOR" C$, "CØMMØN STØCK THE DIVIDEND"
70 PRINT "RATE IS" D2, "PERCENT AND"
75 PRINT "PRICE EARNINGS RATIØ IS" P2
80 END

RUN

TYPE IN CØRPØRATIØN NAME IN ØNE WØRD? GEARØN
TYPE IN CØMMØN STØCK PRICE? 25.00
TYPE IN EARNINGS AND DIVIDEND PER SHARE? 2.50, 1.00
FOR GEARØN CØMMØN STØCK THE DIVIDEND
RATE IS 4.00 PERCENT AND
PRICE EARNINGS RATIØ IS 10.0
```

Example 9 is a complete program using the interactive INPUT statement and showing system and user responses. Note that each INPUT statement is preceded by a PRINT statement (see statement pairs 25 and 30, 35 and 40, and 45 and 50). In each case the system prints out the message, followed by the question mark, as is shown in the output following the RUN command. The system stops after each question mark, until the user types in what is requested (shown here as underlined responses) and advances the teletypewriter to the next line. The system then proceeds through the remainder of the program. Note that in response to lines 25 and 30 a word, GEARØN, is entered; in response to lines 35 and 40 a constant is entered, and lines 45 and 50 require two constants. When all user-computer interaction is completed, the system performs the computations and prints out the results, as shown in the last three lines of output. This is illustrated in the flowchart of Figure 4-1.

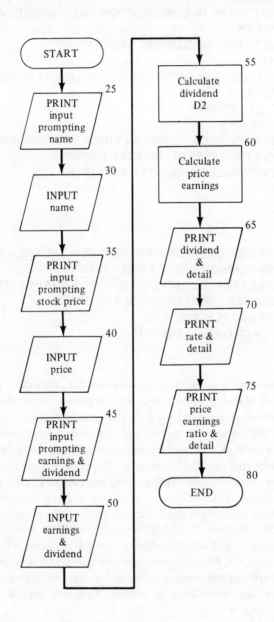

Figure 4-1

SPECIAL STATEMENTS

REM and COMMENT for Documentation

A computer program written by one person is usually difficult for another to interpret, mainly because the variables are not descriptive. In addition, the logic in more complex programs may be difficult to follow.

In order to provide necessary descriptive information, the keyword REM or REMARK can be used. A REM statement informs the system that the statement is there only for documentation and can be ignored.

The Comment approach is another means of inserting information into a program in many systems is to enclose the items in quotation marks (either single or double). Line 130 is an example of BASIC-PLUS comment format. In this method, the exclamation mark is normally used to terminate the executable part of the line and begin the comment part of the line. In other systems, any statement can be used for documentation. A single quotation mark is typed after the statement, and the information is typed after the quotation mark. Examples of such documentation are shown in Example 10.

Example 10

```
20 REM THE VARIABLE A1 STANDS FØR ACTUAL CØST
40 REM A2 = BUDGET, A3 = FIXED CØST
60 REM THIS PRØGRAM CALCULATES TØTAL
80 REM CØST FØR THE SECØND SIX MØNTHS
100 LET X = 1' SETS X EQUAL TØ ØNE
120 IF Y <> X THEN 220' CØMPARES Y AND X
```

The END Statement

The END statement indicates the termination of the program. It must have the highest number in the program and cannot be followed by any other information. It is used to end the program execution and also to signal the BASIC translator that there are no more statements in the program. A STOP statement (discussed in Chapter 5) is a control device to allow conditional jumps determining the actual end of the program.

EXERCISES

1. What is wrong with each of the following BASIC computer program statements?

20 LET S = 18 ÷ 6
30 LET ST = 9.47
40 PRINT k

2. Write a short program to calculate the average of the bid and asked prices of a common stock.

3. Write four different subprograms for reading the numbers 15 and 19 into the numeric variables K and P.

4. Write a program which directs the computer to print out the message that the inventory level of item K is P units, where K and P are numeric variables.

5. Write a program which prints out the digits 0 through 9 in order.

6. Write a LET statement for the following algebraic items:

   a. $Z = (X/Y) + 3$

   b. $Z = \left[\dfrac{2aB}{C + 1} - \dfrac{t}{3(P + T)} \right]^{1/3}$

7. Assign a value of 5.35 to a variable C.

8. Assign the value represented by the variable N to N1.

9. Assign the value 32 to each variable A1, A2, and A3.

10. Print the values of C1, C2, and C3 fifteen spaces apart.

11. Print the values of C1, C2, and C3, printed close together.

12. Show on a sample output how the following will look:

    12 PRINT A1;"TOTAL";TAB (20);A2

13. Show how the input data will look if

    10 INPUT X1,X2,X3,X$
    where:

$X1 = 480 \times 10^{-3}$
$X2 = -5$
$X3 = 1.55$
$X\$ = \text{"APPLE"}$

14. Print the last name, age, and weight of a person in the following format and using the PRINT USING statement.

    XXXXXXX   XXXX   XXX   XX.X

5 BRANCHING AND LOOPING

BRANCHING OR TRANSFER STATEMENTS

In BASIC, as in each programming language, the computer executes a program in the order indicated by the line numbers. However, if one wishes to alter this logical action, a large variety of branching statements (often called transfers) are available. Among the typical statements are the:

1. GØ TØ (or GØTØ)
2. ØN-GØ TØ (or GØTØ) or the Computed GØ TØ (GØTØ)
3. The IF-THEN

The GØ TØ Statement

The GØ TØ statement allows the program to be executed in some other order; it is always followed by the line number to which the system must skip. Having skipped as directed, the computer will then continue to execute the program in the usual order.

The format for the GØ TØ is rather simple:

GØ TØ (or GØTØ) n

The n is the statement number in the program to which control must pass.

Example 1 illustrates the GØ TØ and some of the other statements previously discussed. The program will be executed in the order indicated by the line numbers except where GØ TØ statements indicate otherwise. The order of the program is 20, 30, 60, 80, 180, 200, 100, 150, 220, 300.

Example 1

```
 20 READ X1, X2, Y1, Y2
 30 DATA 5, .4, 6.9, 7.684
 60 LET X = X2 + X1
 80 GØ TØ 180
100 LET Y = Y1 + Y2
150 GØ TØ 220
180 PRINT X
200 GØ TØ 100
220 PRINT Y
300 END
```

The GØ TØ may also be used to repeat certain parts of a program. These branches could be depicted by a series of interlocking steps as shown in the flowchart of Figure 5-1.

An illustration of this branching GØ TØ is given in Example 2. Note, however, that this particular program will continue forever. (Why?) How to get out of such a "loop" will be discussed in the next section.

Example 2

```
20 READ A, B, C
25 DATA 5, 6, 7
30 LET D = A + B − C
40 PRINT D, A
50 LET A = A + 1
60 GØ TØ 30
70 END
```

Rules for the GØ TØ

1. Do not transfer the GØ TØ to a nonexecutable statement.
2. Transfer to a line number (either larger or smaller than the current number).
3. Skip any number of lines in either direction as needed.
4. Some computers allow multiple-statement lines. If this is the case, the GØ TØ should be the last statement on the line.
5. Be aware of the GØ TØ's danger in causing endless loops.

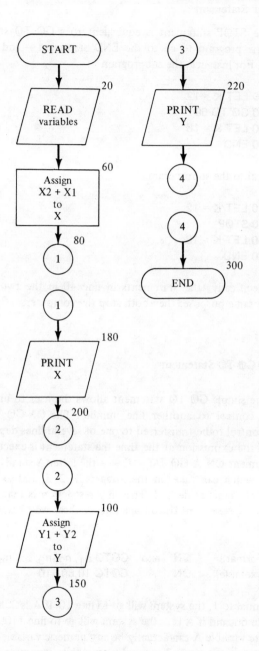

Figure 5-1

The STØP Statement

The STØP statement is equivalent to a GØ TØ statement that directs the program to go to the END statement – and thus end the program. For instance, the subprogram

```
30 LET K = 12
40 GØ TØ 60
50 LET K = 18
60 END
```

is identical to the subprogram

```
30 LET K = 12
40 STØP
50 LET K = 18
60 END
```

Specifically, the statements in line 40 in the two subprograms serve the same purpose: they both stop the computer.

The ØN-GØ TØ Statement

The simple GØ TØ statement allows the user to unconditionally transfer control to another line number. The ØN-GØ TØ statement allows control to be transferred to one of several lines depending on the value of the expression at the time the statement is executed. Consider the statement ØN A GØ TØ ––,––,: the letter A stands for a numeric variable which can take on the integers 1, 2, 3, and so on, up to the number of branches desired. The only restriction is that the ØN A GØ TØ ––,––, statement fits on one line. A three-way branch might look like this:

```
(Format)    ØN   exp   GØTØ n₁, n₂, n₃, ...., nₘ
(Example)   ØN   A     GØTØ 10,60,110
```

If A is equal to 1, the system will go to line 10; if A is 2, the system will go to line 60; and if A is 3, the system will go to line 110.

The variable A can actually be any numeric variable; it can also be an expression. Example 3 is a program which illustrates the use of the ØN statement.

Example 3

```
10 LET J = 1
20 ØN J GØ TØ 30, 60, 70, 90
30 PRINT J
40 LET J = J + 1
50 GØ TØ 20
60 PRINT J
70 LET J = J + 2
80 GØ TØ 20
90 PRINT J
100 END

RUN

1
2
4
```

The program in Example 3 operates as follows: J is set equal to 1 at line 10. At line 30 the value of J (that is, 1) is printed. At line 40 the value of J is increased by one to 2, and at line 50 the system is returned to line 20. At line 20, since J is now equal to 2, the system is directed to line 60, where the new value of J is printed out. The value of J is increased by two to 4 in line 70; at line 80 the system is returned to line 20, where it is told to move to line 90 (because $J = 4$ now). At line 90 the value of J is printed out, and the program moves to the last statement to end the process. The flowchart in Figure 5-2 is drawn in a fashion to show there are four decisions based on the value of J.

The Computed GØ TØ Statement

The Computed GØ TØ, used by some systems, provides a multiple check and one single transfer, based on the truncated value of the expression. The truncated value of the expression is computed and checked for being between one and the number of line numbers. If not between the numbers, this would end the program.

(Format)	GØ TØ $(N_1, N_2, N_3, ..., N_m)$ exp
(Example)	GØ TØ (10,100) I
	INPUT I

N_1, N_2, etc. are line numbers, and the exp is the expression. If the exp is 1, control is transferred to N_1; if 2, to N_2; etc.

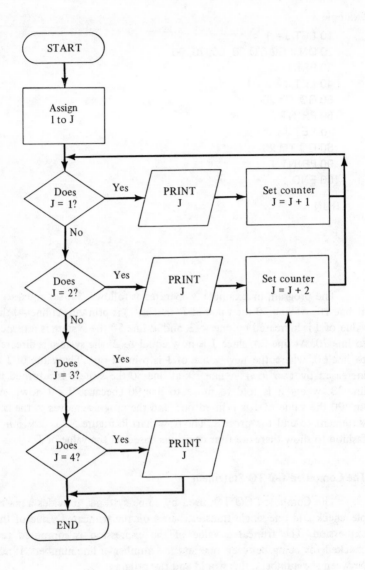

Figure 5-2

The IF-THEN Statement

The IF-THEN statement is a transfer statement suitable for two-way branching. Frequently, an evaluation or comparison must be made in a program. Based on the results of the comparison, the system proceeds in one or another direction. The statements used to make the comparison are the IF--THEN and the IF--GØ TØ statements; either can be used.* In an actual program, the double dash (--) is replaced with a comparison symbol from the following list of relational symbols.

Relational Symbols

It was suggested earlier that relational symbols are useful for making comparisons — which is a key function of a computer. Figure 5-3 shows some common relational symbols.

Math Symbol	English Meaning	Relational Symbol	Example
=	is equal to	=	X=Y
<	is less than	<	X<Y
≤	is less than or equal to	<=	X<=Y
≥	is greater than or equal to	>=	X>=Y
≠	is not equal to	< >	X< >Y

Figure 5-3

Using the IF Statement

The actual statement would look like this:

90 IF X < Y GØ TØ 110

The computer compares the variable or expression to the left of the equal or inequality sign with the variable or expression to the right. If the comparison is true, the system proceeds to the statement whose line number is indicated. If the comparison is not true, the system goes to the statement with the next line number. Example 4 illustrates the BASIC statements.

Example 4

```
  60 IF A = B THEN 180
  70 IF A = B GØ TØ 180
 130 IF X1 < = B THEN 40
 140 IF X1 < = B GØ TØ 40
 500 IF C > D2 THEN 190
 600 IF C > D2 GØ TØ 190
```

*Some systems in the batch mode do not accept the GØ TØ.

Lines 60 and 70 compare the variables A and B; if A is equal to B, the system is directed to move to line 180; if A is not equal to B, the system will automatically move to the next line in the program. Lines 130 and 140 check whether X1 is less than or equal to B; if it is either, the system is directed to line 40. Similarly, in lines 500 and 600 the system is directed to line 190 if C is larger than D2.

Let us now see how we could have gotten out of the loop in Example 2. Suppose we wanted the system to loop 15 times and then stop; we could do this with the following program.

Example 5

```
20 READ A, B, C
25 DATA 5, 6, 7
30 LET D = A + B − C
40 PRINT D, A
45 IF A = 15 THEN 70
50 LET A = A + 1
60 GØ TØ 30
70 END
```

Note that the only difference between Examples 2 and 5 is the statement on line 45. It directs the system to end the computations when A equals 15. The statement

```
45 IF A > = 15 THEN 70
```

will accomplish the same thing; it is also a safer statement to use, because it directs the program to end for every value of A that equals or exceeds 15.

LOOPING STATEMENTS

In almost every program discussed there could be a need for repeating one or more steps. The steps that may be executed more than once, often many times, are part of the looping process. Generally two or more statements are used to accomplish this. This built-in looping facility is provided for by the FØR and NEXT statement pair.

The FØR-NEXT Statement

The loop is fully described by the loop-beginning keyword FØR--TØ − and the loop-ending command NEXT A. In an actual program the double dash is replaced with a formula in which a numeric variable appears to the left of the equal sign, and a constant or expression to the right of the equal sign. The single dash is replaced with a constant or an expression (in this chapter only constants will be used). The A is always the same numeric variable that appears in the FØR--TØ — statement. Thus, the complete statements might appear in a program as

```
40 FØR J = 0 TØ 3
50 NEXT J
```

We illustrate the use of the loop with a short program.

Example 6

```
130 LET X = 0
140 FØR I = 1 TØ 5
150 LET X = X + I
200 NEXT I
250 PRINT "THE VALUE ØF X IS" X
300 END

RUN

THE VALUE ØF X IS 15
```

The loop is comprised of statements 140, 150, and 200; note that the same numeric variable (I) appears in line 140 following FØR and in line 200 following NEXT. The program will repeat line 150 five times, once for each value of I from 1 to 5, as specified in line 140. After looping the specified five times, the system will move to line 250 and print out the final value of the variable X, which is simply the sum of the first five digits.

The loop in Example 6 increases (or steps) the value of the numeric variable I by 1 in each cycle. However, if some other increment is required, the FØR-- TØ — statement can be expanded to include STEP followed by the desired increment. Furthermore, the increment may be negative as well as positive, and the initial value of the numeric variable in the loop may be negative, positive, or zero. Some possible loop configurations are shown below.

Example 7

```
10 FØR X = 0 TØ 4.5 STEP .5
20 NEXT X
```

```
110 FØR Y = 8 TØ 0 STEP −2
120 NEXT Y
210 FØR I = −2.5 TØ 5 STEP 1.5
220 NEXT I
310 FØR J = 2 TØ −2 STEP −1
320 NEXT J
```

In Example 7, lines 10 and 20 form a loop which initially assigns the value of 0 to X. The "STEP .5" command increases the value of X by one-half in each step. Hence the second value of X is .5, the third value is 1.0, and so forth, until the value of X reaches 4.5 at the tenth step.

Another loop is formed by lines 110 and 120. The initial value of Y is 8, and it increases in steps of −2 (i.e., decreases in steps of 2). Hence the second value of Y is 6, the third value is 4, the fourth is 2, and the fifth and final value of Y is 0.

Lines 210 and 220 form a third loop. The initial value of I is −2.5, and it increases in steps of 1.5. Hence, the second value of I is −1, the third is .5, the fourth is 2.0, the fifth is 3.5, and the sixth and final value of I is 5.

The last loop is formed by lines 310 and 320. The first value of J is 2, and it decreases in steps of 1. Hence the second value of J is 1, the third value is 0, the fourth value is −1, and the fifth and final value of J is −2.

If the programmer gives a loop instruction which is impossible to perform, the system will move automatically to the next line following the end of the loop. An example of an incorrect instruction would be the statement in line 310 without the "STEP −1" part. (Why?)

Frequently, loops appear within loops in programs; these are called nested loops. The beginning and ending commands of one loop may be contained within those of another loop, but commands cannot "cross". Figure 5-4 illustrates combinations of loops that are allowed and that are not allowed. The depth of nesting — that is, the number of loops nested — is limited; the programmer should ensure that he does not exceed the capacity of the computer.

Example 8 is a short program with a nested loop.

Example 8

```
10 LET X = Y = 0
20 FØR I = 0 TØ 4 STEP 2
30 FØR J = 10 TØ 8 STEP −1
```

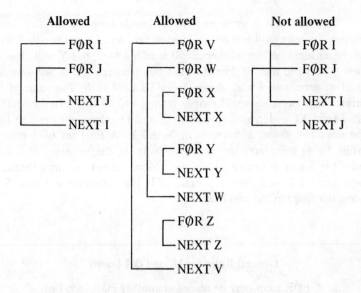

Allowed	Allowed	Not allowed

Figure 5-4
Various Loop Configurations

```
40 LET X = X + I
50 LET Y = Y + J
60 PRINT I, J, X, Y
70 NEXT J
80 NEXT I
90 END

RUN

0    10    0    10
0     9    0    19
0     8    0    27
2    10    2    37
2     9    4    46
2     8    6    54
4    10   10    64
4     9   14    73
4     8   18    81
```

Example 8 is a program with a double loop. In the first pass through the program I will be set equal to zero and J equal to 10. X will not be changed in line 40, because 0 is added to 0, but Y will change from 0 to 10 in line 50. For the next two passes, I and X will remain equal to zero, and J will change from 10 to 9 to 8. The value of Y during these two passes will change from 10 to 19 to 27. In the fourth pass I (and X) is increased from 0 to 2, and J's value is returned to 10. The next two passes increase both X and Y. A final set of 3 passes (while I = 4) completes the iteration. Note, in the printout, that because the J loop is nested within the I loop, the system steps through the values of J once for each value of I. The flowchart in Figure 5-5 shows the range of the two loops.

General Rules for Using FØR Loops

1. A FØR loop may be placed in another FØR loop only if the inner loop is completely within the outer loop.
2. A FØR loop should be entered by first executing the FØR statement. For example, a FØR loop should not be entered from a branching statement that is outside of the loop.
3. Remember that expressions in the FØR statement (such as STEP 2), in most dialects, are evaluated only when executing the FØR statement. Therefore, if statements in the loop change the values of variables that appear in any of the expressions, the loop parameters would remain unchanged for later iterations of the loop.
4. Change the value of the scalar numeric variable (the index of the loop) as needed during execution of the loop.

SUMMARY

FØR loops should be utilized to reduce as much as possible the amount of computer time used. Care should be made to terminate loops properly. Make certain a nested loop is within the correct range. Remember that if a loop is to be executed again, then control is transferred back to the start of the loop. This means that the instructions in the repeated portion do not have to be written more than once.

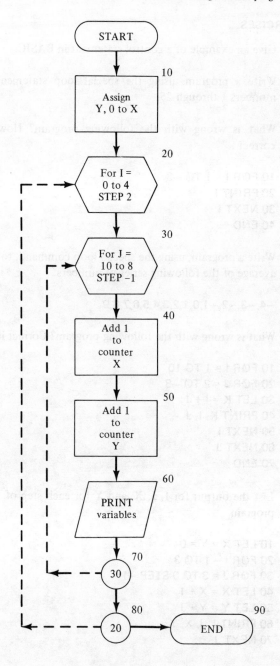

Figure 5-5

EXERCISES

1. Give an example of a control statement in BASIC.

2. Write a program, using the special loop statement, to list the numbers 1 through 25.

3. What is wrong with the following program? How would you correct it?

    ```
    10 FØR I = 1 TØ −3
    20 PRINT I
    30 NEXT I
    40 END
    ```

4. Write a program, using the special loop command, to calculate the average of the following series of numbers:

    −4,−3,−2,−1,0,1,2,3,4,5,6,7,8,9

5. What is wrong with the following program? Correct it.

    ```
    10 FØR I = 1 TØ 10
    20 FØR J = 2 TØ −8
    30 LET K = I + J
    40 PRINT K, I, J
    50 NEXT I
    60 NEXT J
    70 END
    ```

6. List the output for I, J, X, and Y for each step of the following program.

    ```
    10 LET X = Y = 0
    20 FØR I = 1 TØ 3
    30 FØR J = 3 TØ 0 STEP −1
    40 LET X = X + 1
    50 LET Y = Y + J
    60 PRINT I, J, X, Y
    70 NEXT J

    80 NEXT I
    90 END
    ```

7. List the output for X and Y for each step of the following program.

```
10 LET X = Y = 0
20 FØR I = 2 TØ 6 STEP 2
30 FØR J = 10 TØ 0 STEP −5
40 LET Y = Y + J
50 PRINT X, Y
60 NEXT J
70 LET X = X + 1
80 NEXT I
90 END
```

8. What does an IF statement accomplish?

9. What's wrong with this IF statement?

```
100 IF 8 < 9 THEN 150
```

10. Write a program which will compute (1) 7% of $2000 and (2) 8% of $1800 and will determine which is the larger.

11. Several branching and looping statements are shown. Debug these.
    a.   10 ØN T GØ TØ 25
    b.   20 ØN N$ GØ TØ 50,60,70,80
    c.   30 FØR X(I) = 1 TØ 100
    d.   40 FØR I = J TØ K STEP I
    e.   IF X + Y < > Z THEN A
    f.   60 GØ TØ 150 IF J = 3
    g.   IF X THEN Y + 5
    h.   GØ TØ (5,6,7,8)

6 ARITHMETIC OPERATIONS

ALGEBRAIC OPERATIONS AND GENERAL RULES

So far little attention has been given to mathematical operations. This has been done intentionally to enable the reader to focus his attention on the various statements to be mastered before advancing to more difficult programming problems. But now we are ready to discuss the algebraic operations.

The computer performs algebraic operations in the same order as is customary in manual practice. In an expression containing only algebraic signs and symbols, exponentiation is performed first, followed by multiplication and division, and finally by addition and subtraction. For instance, given $A \uparrow X + B * C \uparrow Y$, the system will first raise A to the power X and C to the power Y; next it will multiply B by C^Y; then it will add the terms of the expression.

It is possible to modify the order in which operations are performed in an expression through the use of parentheses.

Special Rules for Parentheses

1. Any formula within parentheses is to be evaluated first.
2. Where parentheses are nested (e.g., $((X + (Y*3)))$, the innermost quantity in a parenthesis is evaluated first.
3. If there are no parentheses, the operations will be performed in the order as indicated above.
4. If there are no parentheses, but the operations are on the same level, the operations are evaluated from left to right.

These rules can be illustrated by the expression

$$(D \uparrow 2 - F)^* ((A + B)^* G) \uparrow 3$$

The system will first add A and B, then multiply by G, and finally raise the result to the third power. Also, F will be subtracted from D^2, and then the remaining multiplication will be performed.

If the system must perform several identical operations, it will do them from left to right in the expression. For instance, in X – Y – Z, the system will subtract Y from X and subtract Z from their difference. Also, given X/Y/Z, the system will divide X by Y and then divide that quotient by Z. For X ↑ Y ↑ Z, the system will raise X to the power Y, and the result to the power Z. If in writing a program, the programmer is not sure of the order the system will follow, he should add sets of parentheses. For instance, (X/Y)/Z will be treated exactly as X/Y/Z. However, X/(Y/Z) will result in a different order of divisions, and hence a different answer.

Special Rules for Arithmetic Operations

1. Never leave out necessary parentheses, and each left parenthesis should have a matching right one.
2. In exponentiation, negative numbers can be raised only to integer powers. Positive can be raised to integer or floating. If an exponent is not an integer, use a log function.
3. Never put two arithmetic operations next to each other. Again, parentheses may be useful to separate them, such as A*(–B).
4. When a symbolic name is used in the expression, then a constant should have been assigned to the name previously.
5. In order to save programming time, be sure to use the available functions (listed later in this chapter).
6. When appropriate, be sure to assign constants to variables by using statements such as LET or READ.

MATHEMATICAL FUNCTIONS

The computer can perform a number of standard mathematical operations directly, without being given detailed instructions. The programmer simply sets a numeric variable equal to the required function as specified by a three-letter name. Such functions save considerable time, especially if they are needed frequently. A summary of some of the most-used functions is presented in Table 6-1. Some additional ones are listed in Appendix B.

Table 6-1. A Summary of Mathematical Functions

Function name	Function description
SQR(X)	Finds the square root of X ($\sqrt{x}$)
LØG(X)	Finds the natural logarithm of X (1n X)
EXP(X)	Finds the value of e (.2718) to the Xth power [e^X or exp (X)]
ABS(X)	Finds the absolute value of X (| x |)
ATN(X)	Finds the arctangent of X in radians
SIN(X)	Finds the sine of X in radians
CØS(X)	Finds the cosine of X in radians
TAN(X)	Finds the tangent of X in radians
CØT(X)	Finds the cotangent of X in radians
INT(X)	Finds the greatest integer less than or equal to X
SGN(X)	Finds the sign of X (prints it as +1, -1, or 0 if X=0)

Some of these mathematical functions, especially the trigonometric, may have limited usefulness in business applications, while others are extremely useful. Several of the functions in Table 6-1 are illustrated in Example 1. Note that the numeric variable in the parentheses following the function name must be assigned a value before any computations can be performed. This example is also depicted in the flowchart of Figure 6-1.

Example 1

```
10 LET X = 6
20 LET Y1 = EXP(X)
30 LET Y2 = LØG(X)
40 LET Y3 = SQR(X)
50 LET X = −6.3
60 LET Y4 = ABS(X)
70 LET Y5 = SGN (X)
80 PRINT Y1, Y2, Y3, Y4, Y5
90 END

RUN

403.429    1.79176    2.44949    6.3    −1
```

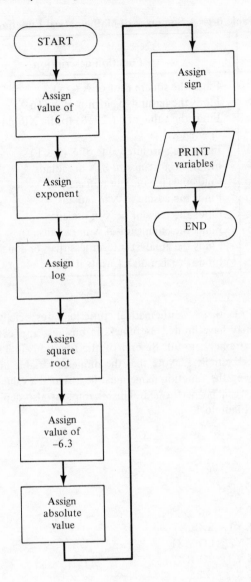

Figure 6-1

SQR Function

In Example 1 we note the SQR function for determining the square root of a number. We naturally could have used a statement such as

10 LET Y3 = 180 ↑ 0.5

corresponding to the algebraic expression $Y = 180^{1/2}$. However, the easiest way is that shown on p. 53:

40 LET Y3 = SQR (180)

This activates another program called SQR, which is stored in memory and calculates anything in the subscript — whether a variable or expression. The item in the subscript is called the "Argument." In similar manner many other functions can be used to advantage such as to round numbers and do many other mathematical operations.

INT Function

The INT function automatically activates a stored program called INT to determine the greatest integer that is less than or equal to X. The X, again, can be any type of item. The common term for this kind of operation is called "truncation." For example, suppose we have a table such as this:

Line No.	X	Y
20	15.9	– 3.9

The values after truncation, using the INT, would be 15. and –4. The negative is the next lower integer.

For rounding, consider the statements

10 LET X = INT (X + .5)
20 LET Y = INT (X + .5)

and the table as above:

30	14.9	87.7

The values after rounding would be 15. and 88.

DEF Function

In addition to the standard functions discussed above, the programmer may specify his own functions by use of the DEF statement. The DEF statement performs a function similar to that of the LET statement; it tells the computer that the program is about to define a variable function. The variable function name consists of three letters, the first two of which are FN; the third letter can be any letter of the alphabet. Following the function name can be any number of numeric variables enclosed in a parenthesis, provided the complete definition fits on one line. The DEF function's versatility is illustrated in Example 2.

Summary of Function Uses and Rules

1. Use a function in an assignment statement, according to the format   LET C = SQR (A ↑ 2 + B ↑ 2).
2. Use a function in a PRINT statement, according to the format   PRINT A, B, SQR (A ↑ 2 + B ↑ 2).
3. Use a function in a mathematical expression, in the format   LET X = 2.345/SQR (2*3.14).
4. Refer to the User's Guide to determine what built-in or library functions are available.
5. Although arguments can contain constants, names, or expressions, they cannot be arguments of themselves.
6. It is a good practice to place the DEF statement at the very beginning of the program — as a nonexecutable statement.
7. Consult your particular system to determine whether you may include more than one argument in user-defined internal functions.

Example 2

```
 5 READ I,J,K,X,Y
10 DEF FNA(I) = INT(I)
20 DEF FNB(J) = J↑3+K
30 DEF FNC (X,Y) = X↑2+2*X*Y+Y↑2
40 DEF FNE (I,J,X,Y) = (FNA(I) + (FNB(J)/FNC(X,Y))
50 DEF FND = Y
55 DATA 5,5,5,5,5
60 END
```

Note in Example 2 that the letters DEF are followed by the function name, an equal sign, and the mathematical definition of the function being specified. The expression to the right of the equal sign may be any expression and may even include other DEF functions previously defined. Previously defined variables and constants may also be used to the right of the equal sign.

The DEF function will typically be used when the programmer expects to use a function a number of times. Instead of repeating the statement each time he uses it, he can simply change the values of the variables involved. In Chapter 11 we discuss subroutines, which perform a function analogous to the DEF statement.

EXERCISES

1.   Write a short program to calculate $f(x) = [\exp(-bx)]/a$, where a = 5, b = 2, and x takes on the integer values from 0 through 3.

2.   Write an efficient computer program to find the maximum positive integer x for which the square root of x is less than 100 and to find the maximum positive integer x for which exp x is less than 100.

3.   When the parentheses are not used in an expression, what operations does the computer do first?

4.   What is an argument? Give an example of its use.

5.   Write a program which will compute $\sqrt{9.9 \times 8.9}$

6.   Write a program which will compute the log of 6.5 + 7.5.

7.   Write the BASIC equivalents of the following algebraic formulas:

   a. $\dfrac{M}{N-2}(2N^2 - 4)$

   b. $R = \dfrac{-B \pm \sqrt{B^2 - 4aC}}{2a}$

8.   Record the sequence of operations for

   A*D**2+B*G**3/C

   List the sequence as steps from a to f.

7 SYSTEM COMMANDS

Commands cause BASIC to perform certain computer operations immediately. Typical commands instruct the computer to run and save programs. Since they are special messages to communicate with the computer, instead of instructions used in problem solutions, they do not require line numbers.

General Rules for Commands

1. Omit all line numbers from commands.
2. Terminate each command with the Return key.
3. Consult the user's guide for the terminal to obtain the command list.

There are no standard control cards in BASIC since they are independent of the language — so commands must be used for the particular operating system. They are often placed at the start of the program.

TYPICAL SYSTEM COMMANDS

RUN

As a special message to the computer, one of the most essential types to use would involve the use of the word RUN. This word tells the computer you have completed typing the program and you will now want to execute it (convert to machine language). Running the program does not mean that the logical output is completely correct. Rather, the computer indicates there are no serious clerical errors present. Although the RUN command is standard in all systems, many of the other commands have variations. Following are some that are most standard.

NEW

If you want to type a new program with a new name, you can use the command NEW. The coding would look like that shown in Example 1.

Example 1

```
NEW
NEW PROGRAM NAME-XYZ

READY
```

In some systems the computer merely erases the old program. Other systems require the word SCRATCH with the command NAME, followed by the new name. Some systems limit the program name length.

LIST

The command LIST prints all the statements in the working area of the computer. On many systems the command can be abbreviated to LIS. If you type LIST (or LIS), your program will be printed as it was typed. On a few systems, the listing begins with the name of the program. Also, if you qualify the command with a line number following it, only the lines after this are printed.

Example 2

```
    LIST 10
    10 LET Y = 5
    20 PRINT X,Y
    30 END
    READY
```

In Example 2 only lines 10 and following are printed. If the listing had been

```
    LIST 10,20
```

then only lines 10 to 20 could be printed, and not line 30. None of the lines not printed are destroyed.

SAVE, OLD, and UNSAVE

To save a program for future use, the SAVE command takes the particular program from the working area and copies it into the storage area of the computer. Any program so stored stays there until erased; the CØPY action does not erase the program. The number of programs so stored depends on the size of the particular computer. The program would look like the one in Example 3.

Example 3

```
NEW
NEW PRØGRAM NAME- XYZ
READY
10 PRINT A,B,C
20 END
SAVE
READY (indicates the program XYZ has been saved)
```

Now we can request program XYZ by typing ØLD. The computer may type back ØLD PRØGRAM NAME – and then we would supply XYZ. The computer takes the program from the storage area and puts it in the working area. After the resulting READY, we merely type RUN. Since it is now in the working area, we can now use the LIST if we desire it.

To erase a program from the working storage area, we type the command UNSAVE. This command erases a program in storage – a program with the same name as the one in the working area. To check to see if it has been erased, we request the program to determine if "PRØGRAM NAME NØT FØUND".

Example 4

```
NEW
NEW PRØGRAM NAME- XYZ
READY
UNSAVE
READY
ØLD
ØLD PRØGRAM NAME-XYZ
PRØGRAM NAME NØT FØUND
READY
```

CATALOG or CAT

Many systems have a method of identifying the programs saved in the working storage. All the programs saved can be printed out by the command CATALØG (CAT).

DELETE

In order to erase unwanted statements, we normally use a DELETE command followed by the line number to be erased. The command

DELETE 10–20

would erase all items from line 10 through line 20. On many systems if only one line number follows the DELETE, only that line is erased. After the lines are deleted, the READY appears.

RENUMBER or REN

The RENUMBER command is useful in some systems to resequence the line numbers. After the READY is typed, the out-of-sequence numbers are renumbered, as in Example 5.

Example 5

```
    RENUMBER
    READY
    LIST
    10 LET X = 5
    20 LET Y = 10
    30 PRINT X,Y
    40 END
    READY
```

Then to examine the listing, just type LIST.*

TO ALTER A PROGRAM IN STORAGE

First it is necessary to copy the old program from storage to the working areas. To alter, for example, a PRINT A statement, we could do as shown in Example 6.

---

*Some systems use a RESEQUENCE command.

Example 6

```
10 PRINT A        (The alteration)
   LIST           (To check to see if the alteration was com-
                  pleted)
10 PRINT A
20 PRINT B
30 END
   READY
   REPLACE        (used to replace the old version)
   READY
```

RENAME

To rename, use the RENAME command followed by a new name, as shown in Example 7.

Example 7

```
NEW
NEW PRØGRAM NAME- REP1
10 PRINT 1*2*3
20 END
   SAVE
   PRØGRAM NAME HAS BEEN USED
   READY
   RENAME P
   READY
   SAVE
   READY
```

COMMANDS TO TERMINATE

At the end of a program the computer will print READY, and we type one of the approved exits from the program. One of the commonly used such commands is BYE, which signals that we are now logging out. The command would be simply

```
RUN
SALES = 5
READY
BYE
```

The significance of this command can be illustrated by the fact that any program we developed to compute SALES previously is now destroyed. In other words, it logs us out and erases everything in the entire working area.

EXERCISES

1. If a program actually RUNS, can you be sure the results you receive are correct?

2. What are the BASIC systems commands in use in your school or office? Familiarize yourself with those not discussed in this chapter.

3. What does the computer ask for if you don't give it a file name when responding to this question:

    NEW or ØLD?

4. How should you select a file name for a new program?

5. Prepare a typical conversation the user would have with the computer when the program is ØLD and it must be unsaved.

6. What is the importance of the LIST command?

7. Given the following BASIC Program:

    ```
    10 LET X = 3
    20 LET Y = (X+3)/6
    30 PRINT X , Y
    40 LET X = 4
    50 LET Y = (X+3)/6
    60 PRINT X , Y
    70 END
    ```

    On your computer, what system commands would you use to process this program? On your computer, how would you delete lines 20 to 50? On your computer, how could you rename the program?

8.   What does each of the following do?
    a.   NEW
    b.   SCRATCH
    c.   ØLD
    d.   UNSAVE
    e.   REPLACE

9.   Write the system commands you would use to delete lines 10 to 30 in the BASIC program in Exercise 7, then renumber each line in the altered program so that the line numbers begin at 10 and increase by 10. Finally, list the resulting program.

8 SUBSCRIPTS AND ARRAYS

SUBSCRIPTED VARIABLES

Subscripted variables increase greatly the number of available numeric variables and are of considerable use when large amounts of data must be handled. A numeric subscripted variable consists of one of the twenty-six letters of the alphabet followed by a set of parentheses which contain one or more numeric variables or one or more constants separated by commas. For instance, (B9) is a specific one-dimensional numeric variable, whereas B(I) stands for a family of subscripted one-dimensional B variables. By letting I take on different values, numerous B variables can be generated and efficiently processed in a program.

Subscripted variables are indispensable when one must deal with a large number of variables. As an example, if a list of constants must be sorted in ascending or descending order, the use of subscripts facilitates the process greatly. As you may recall, without subscripted variables the number of variables is limited to 286. With subscripted variables, letter-digit combinations can no longer be used, but all 26 letters can be subscripted. Thus, subscripts significantly increase the number of available variables.

The following are some typical subscripted variables:

Legal	Illegal
A (3)	(4.32)
A (K)	A (XX)
P (2*A–B)	A (#B)
P(1, 3)	

Note that they must consist of one variable only, one numeric, a subscripted variable, or expression. Some systems provide truncation of any floating point numbers. For example, A(2.5) would be truncated to A(2). Suppose we have

Line No.	X(1)	X(2)	X(3)
10	10	11	12

and we generate the following statements:

```
10  DATA 10, 11, 12
20  READ X(1), X(2), X(3)
30  LET Y = X (1) + X(2) + X(3)
40  PRINT Y, X(1), X(2), X(3)
50  END
```

After line 20 is executed, X(1) has a value of 10, X(2) has 11, and X(3) has 12. What distinguishes one variable name from the other appears in the subscript.

Subscript as a Variable

Typical statements of the subscripted variable could be

```
READ X(A)
PRINT X (A)
```

The subscript A is now a variable. If the value was 2, this is the same as if it were A(2). The variable names, as mentioned, are not important; if two variables have the same value, either can be used.

Subscripts as Accumulators

By means of the FOR loop, in conjunction with a program to set up an indexing control, we can utilize subscripts on an accumulator basis. Such statements are illustrated in Example 1; see also the flow-chart in Figure 8-1.

Example 1

```
10 DATA 10, 11, 12
20 LET X = 0
30 FØR K = 1 TØ 3
40 READ Y(K)
50 LET X = X + Y(K)
60 NEXT K
70 PRINT X
```

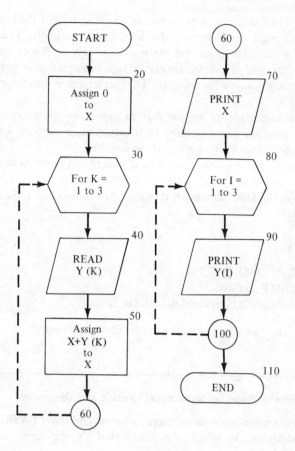

Figure 8-1

```
80 FØR I = 1 TØ 3
90 PRINT Y(I)
100 NEXT I
110 END
```

THE DIM STATEMENT

The DIM (for DIMENSIØN) statement must appear in a program that includes subscripted variables, numeric or string (the latter to be discussed in Chapter 10), whose subscripts exceed 10. Subscripts with a value of 10 or less need not be shown. In a DIM statement the keyword DIM is followed by a list of the subscripted variables. The DIM statement is required to instruct the system to save sufficient space in the computer, and it usually appears at the beginning of a program. When matrix keywords are used, the DIM statement is mandatory (see Chapter 9).

It is important to realize that in order for the computer to process a program that has subscripted variables, a memory location must be reserved for each element of the variable.

Numeric variables can have several dimensions (some systems are limited to two dimensions only) which must, of course, be properly indicated in the DIM statement. Example 2 contains three typical DIM statements.

Example 2

```
10 DIM C(45), D (5,25)
20 DIM F (5,6,20)
30 DIM S$(5) (Discussed in Chapter 10)
```

Question: How much space is reserved by these statements?

General Rules for Subscripts (Variable and Dimension)

1. Dimension statements occur prior to any other BASIC statement in which the subscripted variable name is used.
2. If no dimensions are given, only 10 cells are provided for each vector.
3. The use of a variable in the dimension, such as DIM A(K), is to be avoided.
4. Variables are allowed one or two subscripts.
5. It is possible to use, in some systems, the same variable name as both a subscripted and an unsubscripted variable.
6. Although the DIM statement can be placed anywhere in the program, and anywhere in a multiple-statement line, it is good practice to put them at the first to make easy alterations.

ARRAYS

Variables, as mentioned, can be subscripted to enable one variable name to represent many quantities. If we were using a compound-interest formula to prepare a series of 40 different rates of interest, it would be difficult to name each one. The 40 rates, in this case, constitute an array.

We can refer to the entire array by one variable name, and we can refer to each element in the array in terms of its position in that array. A typical example is shown in Example 3.

Example 3

```
100 DIM A (5)
110 LET A (3) = 4.1
```

This program segment first sets aside 5 elements called A. Then it assigns the value 4.1 to the third element. After these instructions are executed, the A values look like this:

```
A
0
0
4.1
0
0
```

Arrays may contain thousands of elements, depending on the particular computer system. Values can be assigned by the DATA statement to each element, as in Example 4.

Example 4

```
10 DIM A(5)
20 FØR K = 1 TØ 5
30 READ A(K)
40 NEXT K
50 DATA 1,2,3,4,5
```

Reverse-Order Arrays

Having placed the five values above in an array and having the five lines printed, we will want to print them in reverse order on occasion. The statements shown in Example 5 will accomplish this.

Example 5

```
10 FØR X = 1 TØ 5
20 PRINT Y(6-X)
30 NEXT X
40 END
```

In this partial program, it can be seen that X contains the value 1; and when statement 10 is executed, 6-X gives the value 5. When X changes to 2, 6-X changes to 4, etc. This process reverses the array.

Sorting with Arrays

The BASIC language is a rather common approach to sorting. Different useful programs can be written to supply a method for each particular application. One useful technique would be the bubble sort. The complete program can't be allotted sufficient coverage in an introductory text. However, briefly, the procedure would be to take a set of random numbers, and assuming we wanted to place these numbers in ascending order, we would start from the bottom. If the numbers are already in ascending sequence, they stay the same — otherwise, they are reversed. Each item can be compared with the other, as a pair. A BASIC program to do this would necessarily include a combination of FØR statements to (a) count the maximum number of passes needed to sort the complete series of random numbers and (b) make comparisons (using IF statements). The array would then be

A
1
2
3
4
5

Two-Dimensional Arrays

Doubly subscripted numeric variables can be thought of as forming a matrix of constants, where the first subscript represents the number of a row and the second subscript the number of a column in the matrix. For instance, the array

$$\begin{bmatrix} 5 & 4 & 3 & 2 \\ 6 & 1 & 9 & 7 \\ 8 & 2 & 1 & 5 \end{bmatrix}$$

can be represented by the one general doubly subscripted numeric variable $B(I, J)$, where $I = 1$, 2, or 3 to represent each of the three rows and $J = 1$, 2, 3, or 4 to represent each of the four columns. The twelve constants are then denoted by the doubly subscripted variable as follows: $B(1,1) = 5$, $B(1,2) = 4$, $B(1,3) = 3$, $B(1,4) = 2$, $B(2,1) = 6$, $B(2,2) = 1,..., B(3,4) = 5$.

Subscripted variables with more than two subscripts are more difficult to define in terms of lists or matrices. However, they are very useful for recording attributes of individuals or things. Suppose, for example, that we wanted to record the information in the table below, using a subscripted variable. Let the first subscript be education (degree or no degree), the second subscript income level ($A = \$10,000$ and $B = \$20,000$), and the third subscript residence (city or suburban). The summary table could then be recorded in the triply subscripted variable $A(I, J, K)$ as follows: $A(1,1,1) = 5$, $A(1,1,2) = 10$, $A(1,2,1) = 10$, $A(1,2,2) = 30$, $A(2,1,1) = 10$, $A(2,1,2) = 5$, $A(2,2,1) = 15$, and $A(2,2,2) = 15$.

	City		Suburban	
Education	A	B	A	B
Degree	5	10	10	30
No Degree	10	15	5	15

EXERCISES

1. Which of the following DIM statements are incorrect? In what way?

    ```
    10 DIM H(5),H6(I)
    20 DIM J(6),K(4),T(7,6)
    30 DIM K( ),F$(4)
    40 DIM J$(4,3),P(16,14,5),B(4)
    ```

2. What does the DIM statement accomplish?

3. If a program contains the statement

    ```
    10 DIM R(50)
    ```

    what values do subscripts take in the program?

4. Read the following values into an array named X. Then have the program print the values.

    10 DATA 8,42,21,25,20

5. Read the five values in Exercise 4, then copy the values into an array named Y. Print out the Y values.

6. Refer to Exercise 4. Read the same values in and have the computer find the smallest value in the array.

7. As a class project, do the following, using values from Exercise 4.
    a.   Copy X into A, having the values print in reverse order.
    b.   Reprint X, having the values printed out in ascending order.

8. Print the output for the following program.

    10 READ A,B,C,X,Y
    20 DATA 5,6,4,2,3
    30 LET Z = A↑ X + B*C↑ 4
    40 LET P = (A−B ↑ 2)*((A+B)*C) ↑ 2
    50 LET Q = A/B/C
    60 LET R = X ↑ Y ↑ 2
    70 LET S = A/(B/C)
    80 PRINT Z,P,Q,R,S
    90 END

9. Write a program to calculate z according to the following formula. Assign the proper numeric variables. Let $a = 3$, $b = 9$, $x = 7$, $y = 6$, and $c = 5$ when you "run" your program.

    $$z = (a+b)^2 - [(x+y)/c]^3 \, [a^{2b}] + [1/a]^2$$

9 MATRIX OPERATIONS

The BASIC computer programming language has built-in features which allow for easy matrix manipulations. Although it is possible to write programs for matrix computations, the availability of special statements for this purpose simplifies the programmer's task considerably.

In this chapter we shall first discuss the various matrix operations, and then illustrate how they are performed. The reader not familiar with matrix and vector operations is referred to Appendix A for a review of this topic.

BASIC may define the size of a matrix in two ways:

1. By including this in a dimension statement using the DIM keyword. The dimensioning establishes the maximum number of elements in each row and column and the maximum of the entire matrix.

2. By not using the DIM, with the assumption that the size of the matrix has 10 elements for a single dimension and 10×10 for a two-dimensional type.

First we will discuss the more normal type, using the DIM statement. The general rules for the use of this statement in matrices are as follows:

1. Only integer values can be used to define the size of a matrix.
2. The size and number of matrices depend on the computer storage available in a particular system.
3. The DIM can be placed anywhere in the program, if necessary. It is often, however, the first statement in the program.
4. Until assigned a value, the first element of the matrix must be zero.
5. Multiple matrices, when defined by a single DIM statement, must be separated by commas.

THE MATRIX OPERATORS

Suppose we want to perform some operation (addition, multiplication, inversion, scalar multiplication, or whatever) on matrices A and B below:

$$A = \begin{bmatrix} 5 & 11 & 14 \\ 12 & 3 & 9 \\ 4 & 12 & 19 \end{bmatrix} \qquad B = \begin{bmatrix} 11 & 4 & 19 \\ 12 & 7 & 9 \\ 9 & 18 & 17 \\ 4 & 6 & 3 \end{bmatrix}$$

Before we can do anything with the matrices, we must enter them into the computer. This can be accomplished with the program in Example 1.

Example 1
```
10 DIM A(3,3),B(4,3)
20 MAT READ A,B
30 DATA 5,11,14,12,3,9,4,12,19
40 DATA 11,4,19,12,7,9,9,18,17,4,6,3
50 END

RUN
```

Note that the first statement in Example 1 is a dimension (DIM) statement. Every program that treats matrices must specify the sizes of the matrices involved, using a DIM statement, unless by default. If there are no dimensions given, only ten cells are provided for each vector or

10 X 10 spaces are provided for each undimensioned matrix. The size of a matrix is determined by the number of rows and the number of columns, given in that order. Since matrix A has three rows and three columns, it is dimensioned as A(3,3). Matrix B has four rows and three columns and is therefore dimensioned as B(4,3). The process of entering the data — that is, the constants making up the matrices — begins with line 20, the MAT READ command. The constants are then entered in row-wise sequence by ordinary DATA statements (lines 30 and 40). Any number of DATA statements can be used, as long as the rows are listed in order, beginning with the first row of the first matrix in the MAT READ statement, and ending with the last row of the last matrix. Since the program in Example 1 has no PRINT statement, there will be no output.

Example 2 illustrates the MAT PRINT statement, which allows previously entered or computed matrices to be printed out in matrix format. Note that matrix A is entered with the MAT READ and DATA statements of lines 20 and 30. Lines 40 and 50 both direct the system to print out matrix A, but in different forms. The semicolon in line 50 indicates that the matrix should be close-packed, as shown in the output below the program. For normal spacing the MAT PRINT statement in line 40 is used.

Example 2

```
10 DIM A(3,3)
20 MAT READ A
30 DATA 5,11,14,12,3,9,4,12,19
40 MAT PRINT A
50 MAT PRINT A;
60 END

RUN
```

5	11	14
12	3	9
4	12	19

5	11	14
12	3	9
4	12	19

Example 3 illustrates two commands which perform operations on matrices. In line 30, matrix A of Example 1 is used to create a new

matrix B exactly like A. Then, in line 40, matrix A is added to matrix B
to form matrix C. Finally, in line 50, matrix B is subtracted from
matrix A to form matrix D. Line 55 then directs the system to print
out matrices C and D. Note in lines 20 through 55 that each matrix
command begins with the letters MAT.

Example 3

```
10 DIM A(3,3),B(3,3),C(3,3),D(3,3)
20 MAT READ A
30 MAT B = A
40 MAT C = A + B
50 MAT D = A − B
55 MAT PRINT C,D
60 DATA 5,11,14,12,3,9,4,12,19
70 END

RUN

10    22    28
24    6     18
8     24    38

0     0     0
0     0     0
0     0     0
```

Multiplying one matrix by another requires that the number of
columns in the first matrix be equal to the number of rows in the
second matrix. Example 4 illustrates not only matrix multiplication,
but also inversion and transposition.

Example 4

```
10 DIM P(2,2),Q(2,2),R(2,3),X(2,3),Y(2,2),Z(2,2)
20 MAT READ P,Q,R
30 DATA 4,3,2,5,1,3,2,4
40 DATA 8,7,4,3,9,6
50 MAT X = P*R
60 MAT Y = INV(Q)
70 MAT Z = TRN(P)
75 MAT PRINT X,Y,Z
80 END

RUN
```

41	55	34
31	59	38

−2	1.5
1	−.5

4	2
3	5

Lines 20, 30 and 40 enter the data for matrices P, Q and R, following the DIM statement on line 10. Line 50 then multiplies matrix P by matrix R and stores the resultant matrix as matrix X. Line 60 takes the inverse of the matrix Q and stores the result as matrix Y, and line 70 takes the transpose of matrix P and stores the result as matrix Z. Note that the matrix-inverse command uses the INV(−) function, and the matrix-transpose command uses the TRN(−) function.

Multiplying each element of a matrix by a scalar (or constant) is accomplished by the command illustrated by line 50 in Example 5. The numeric variable K enclosed in parentheses stands for the value by which each element in the matrix is to be multiplied. Line 50 instructs the system to multiply matrix A by the current value of K and store the result as matrix B. To differentiate it from a matrix K, the numeric variable K must be enclosed in parentheses. Any nonsubscripted numeric variable could, of course, be used in place of K.

Example 5
```
10 DIM A(3,4),B(3,4)
20 MAT READ A
30 DATA 5,6,11,4,2,12,9,7,6,10,8,2
40 LET K=3
50 MAT B=(K)*A
60 MAT PRINT B
70 END

RUN
```

15	18	33	12
6	36	27	21
18	30	24	6

The three statements illustrated in Example 6 conclude our list of the common matrix types. The first one, MAT D = CØN, in line 20, sets each element of matrix D equal to 1; the statement for line 30, MAT E = ZER, sets each element of matrix E equal to zero; and the statement for line 40, MAT F = IDN, sets the diagonal elements of the matrix F equal to 1's, and the remaining elements equal to 0, yielding an identity matrix.

Example 6

```
10 DIM D(2,3),E(3,3),F(3,3)
20 MAT D = CØN
30 MAT E = ZER
40 MAT F = IDN
50 MAT PRINT D,E,F
60 END

RUN

1    1    1
1    1    1

0    0    0
0    0    0
0    0    0

1    0    0
0    1    0
0    0    1
```

MATRIX WITHOUT THE DIM

As mentioned previously, a matrix operation can be defined in one case without the DIM statement. For example, the statement

```
10 MAT X (P,N)
```

without the DIM would be equivalent to

```
10 DIM X (10,10)
```

SPECIAL FEATURES OF MATRIX COMMANDS

The DIM statement indicates what the maximum dimensions of a matrix are. In all our previous examples, it also indicated the exact dimensions. However, it is possible to change the dimension of a matrix in a program, provided the new dimension is equal to or smaller than that specified in the DIM statement. For instance, in Example 6, matrix D was specified to be a 2 X 3 matrix, with 2 rows and 3 columns. However, any matrix of smaller size could be entered with an expanded MAT READ statement. Thus, to make matrix D a 2 X 2 matrix even though it is specified in the DIM statement as a 2 X 3, we would enter the statement

```
15 MAT READ D(2,2)
```

Similarly, three other MAT statements can be used to redimension a matrix. In terms of Example 6, these are:

```
10 MAT D = CØN(2,2)
20 MAT E = ZER(2,2)
30 MAT F = IDN(2,2)
```

Line 30 may also be written as MAT F = IDN(2), because an identity matrix is always a square matrix, that is, a matrix with equal numbers of rows and columns.

Errors seem to crop up readily in MAT statements, and the programmer should be very careful when specifying operations on matrices. For instance, only matrices of identical sizes can be added or subtracted. When two matrices are to be multiplied, the number of columns of the premultiplier — the first matrix in the multiplication formula to the right of the equal sign — must be the same as the number of rows of the postmultiplier, the last matrix in the formula. The size of the resultant matrix must be equal to or smaller than the DIM specifications. As a matter of fact, an error results whenever a matrix is operated on whose dimensions exceed those specified by the DIM statement.

Vectors may be operated upon like matrices, but the same rules must be applied to them. A vector is, in fact, a matrix that has only one row or one column. An eight-element row vector named B is identified as B(1,8), and an eight-element column vector named B is identified as B(8,1). If both these vectors were to be used in a program with the B identification, then at least the following size (DIM) statement would be required:

```
10 DIM B(8,8)
```

Example 7 is a short program illustrating the use of compatible matrices. In line 40 we multiply B times A. Note that, because of their dimensions, we cannot multiply A times B. Similarly, matrices B and D are of identical size, as are matrices A and C, so the former can be subtracted on line 50, and the latter added on line 60.

Example 7

```
10 DIM A(3,1),B(3,3),C(3,1),D(3,3),E(3,3)
20 MAT C = ZER(2,1)
30 MAT READ A(3,1),B(3,3)
40 MAT C = B*A
50 MAT E = B − D
60 MAT B = A + C
70 END
```

In some systems, the same matrix may be placed on both sides of a MAT equation in the case of replacement, addition, subtraction, or scalar multiplication, but not in any other situation. Allowed forms are

```
10 MAT X = X
20 MAT X = X + Y
30 MAT X = (3)*X
40 MAT X = Y − X
```

(Note that the first statement is redundant and therefore not very useful.) The following forms will result in error statements:

```
10 MAT X = X*Y
20 MAT X = INV(X)
30 MAT X = TRN(X)
```

When adding or subtracting, a maximum of two matrices may be used to the right of the equal sign in a formula. For instance,

```
50 MAT A = A − B − C
```

is not allowed. Two statements must be used to accomplish these operations, as follows:

```
60 MAT A = A − B
70 MAT A = A − C
```

In finding the inverse of a matrix, it is frequently desirable to know the value of the determinant of the original matrix. This can be accomplished by following the inverse statement with the determinant statement, as follows:

```
40 MAT D = INV(R)
70 LET S = DET
```

The value of the determinant of matrix R will be stored in S. One can thus determine whether the determinant is large enough for the inverse to be meaningful. If a singular matrix is inverted, the determinant is set equal to zero.*

Example 8 illustrates several of the features of matrix operations discussed so far. Note that the dimensions of matrices can be indicated in MAT statements by numeric variables which, of course, have to be identified; however, numeric variables cannot be used in DIM statements. Also note the use of semicolons in lines 60 and 110 to cause the matrices to be closer packed when they are printed out.

Example 8

```
 10 DIM A(5,5),B(5,5),C(5,5),D(5,5),E(5,5),F(5,5)
 15 DIM G(5,5),H(5,5)
 20 READ I,J
 30 MAT READ A(I,I),B(I,I),D(I,J),G(J,I)
 40 MAT C = ZER(I,I)
 50 PRINT "MATRIX A ØF ØRDER" I
 60 MAT PRINT A;
 70 PRINT "MATRIX B ØF ØRDER" I
 80 MAT PRINT B
 90 MAT C = A + B
100 PRINT "C = A + B"
110 MAT PRINT C;
120 MAT F = ZER(I,J)
130 MAT F = C*D
140 MAT H = ZER(J,J)
150 MAT H = G*F
160 PRINT "MATRIX H ØF ØRDER" J
170 MAT PRINT H
180 DATA 3,1
190 DATA 1,2,3,4,5,6,7,8,9,9,8,7,6,5,4,3,2,1,1,2
```

*A typical BASIC-PLUS example is
40 MAT D = INV (R): D1 = DET
70 MAT E = INV (S): D2 = DET
80 1F D1 = D2 GO TO 80

```
195 DATA 3,3,2,1
200 END

RUN

MATRIX A ØF ØRDER 3

1    2    3
4    5    6
7    8    9
MATRIX B ØF ØRDER 3

9         8         7
6         5         4
3         2         1
C = A + B

10   10   10
10   10   10
10   10   10
MATRIX H ØF ØRDER 1

360
```

MAT INPUT STATEMENT

Some systems make effective use of a special statement called MAT INPUT. This statement is used to input each value of the elements of a predimensioned matrix. Input is read from the keyboard, as it is with the usual input statement, and a ? is printed when the program is ready to accept the input.

The MAT INPUT statement allows input of integer, floating point, and string data, depending on the type of variable name. More than one matrix can be inputted by separating the names by a comma, as shown here.

```
10 DIM A (20), B (20)
20 MAT INPUT A,B
```

VECTOR STATEMENTS

Vectors may be entered into a program by use of the MAT INPUT V statement in some systems (See Appendix B). The number of components in a vector need be specified only if it exceeds 10; a DIM statement is used to specify dimensions in excess of 10. Normally, the elements of a vector are limited in number by what can be typed on one line. However, if the last element on a line is followed by the symbol & (before carriage return, of course), the system will ask for more input on the next line. The system counts the vector elements as they are entered and stores the number of vector elements in the function NUM.

Example 9 illustrates how a 15-element vector is entered, and how the average of its elements is calculated and printed out. Note that several vectors may be entered consecutively and their averages calculated. When no more vectors remain, a carriage return, which has the same effect as setting N equal to zero, will end program execution.

Example 9

```
10 DIM V(15)
20 LET S = 0
30 MAT INPUT V
40 LET N = NUM
50 IF N = 0 THEN 200
60 FØR I = 1 TØ N
70 LET S = S + V(I)
80 NEXT I
90 PRINT "THE AVERAGE ØF THE VECTØR ELEMENTS IS"
100 PRINT S/N
110 GØ TØ 20
200 END

RUN

? 11,14,6,3,9,8,9,15,4,7,1,3,5,6,4
THE AVERAGE ØF THE VECTØR ELEMENTS IS
7
?
```

EXERCISES

1.   Find the errors in the following program and correct them.

    10 DIM X(2,2),Y(3,3),A(3,4)
    20 MAT READ X,Y
    30 MAT A = X + Y
    40 MAT B = Y*A
    50 DATA 0,1,2,3,4,5,6,7,8,9,10
    60 END

2.   Write a program which will check whether the inverse of a 4 X 4 matrix premultiplied by the original matrix results in the 4 X 4 identity matrix.

3.   Write a program to add two eight-element vectors using the MAT operators.

4.   Find the errors in the following statements and correct them.

    10 MAT X = Y
    20 MAT Y = Y + X − B
    30 MAT X = X*Y
    40 MAT B = TRN(X)
    50 MAT A = INV(A)
    60 MAT C = (K)*C
    70 MAT X = A − X

5.   Write a program to find the determinant of a 2 X 5 matrix multiplied by a 5 X 2 matrix. What are the dimensions of the new matrix?

6.   What must you include in your program to have close-packed matrices printed out?

7.   Find the mean and variance of the elements of a ten-element vector with a BASIC program. The formula for the variance is

$$\sum_{i=1}^{n} \frac{(v(i) - \overline{v})^2}{n}$$

8.   Write a program to find the largest element of an eight-element vector.

10 CHARACTER STRINGS

Much of the treatment of BASIC operations has previously involved numeric information. The language, however, also offers a method to handle characters of all kinds. This type of information is called "character string," or "alphanumeric string," or just "string." A string in BASIC is expressed by enclosing any valid BASIC symbol between a pair of double quotation marks. Examples of character strings are

        "HELLO, WHAT SYSTEM IS THIS?"
        "FEBRUARY 1979"
        "**************"

STRING CONSTANTS

Just as numbers can be used as constants, or referenced by variable names, character strings may also do this. Such constants must be in either single or double quotes (or single apostrophe, depending on the system). For example, consider the following strings.

        10 IF A$ = "SUM" GØ TØ 20
        20 LET B$ = "FILE 1"
        30 C$ = 'SAVE''

The constants are "SUM", "FILE 1", and 'SAVE'.

STRING VARIABLES

A string variable, in contrast to a numeric variable, can take on alphanumeric data, a name, or some identifying information. The purpose of string variables is thus to store nonnumeric data in the program and to allow the system to operate on these nonnumeric data.

The name of a string can be any one of the letters of the alphabet, followed by a dollar sign. Typical examples of the string are A$, B$, S$, and Z$, which might stand for the words alpha, beta, sigma, and zeta. In Example 1 the equal signs are used to set the string variable on the left equal to the numeric variable, constant, word, or string variable on the right.

Example 1

```
T$ = "MILK"
A$ = "GØØD"
P$ = R$
```

It is also possible to subscript the string variable as in B$(4), H$(J), and Z$(29). Multiple string variables are not allowed. Subscripted strings must be dimensioned with the DIM statement if the number of subscripts to be used for a given variable exceeds ten.

Many of the keywords used with numeric variables can also be used with string variables, as illustrated in Example 2.

Example 2

```
10 DIM R$(15), D(26,5), H$(30), P(60)
20 LET P$ = "AGE"
30 LET H$(10) = P$
40 IF R$(10) = "WEIGHT" THEN 150
50 IF R$(15) = P$ THEN 160
60 IF "HEIGHT" = H$(25) THEN 170
```

Statement 10 illustrates how numeric and string variables can be mixed in a DIM statement. Line 20 assigns the string AGE to the string variable P$. Note that the string itself must appear in double quotation marks; therefore the marks may never be part of an actual string. In line 30 one string variable is set equal to another string variable; it is irrelevant that one is subscripted and the other is not. Line 40 compares the string in string variable R$10 with the actual string WEIGHT. In line 60 a string is compared with a string variable, and in line 50 two string variables are compared.

Strings may be entered into the computer by the READ or INPUT statements and printed out with the PRINT statement. Example 3 illustrates how this is accomplished. Note that strings and numeric data can be intermixed.

Example 3

```
60 READ P$, A1, R$, Q$
80 DATA IS, 29, YØUR, AGE
100 IF R$ = "ØUR" THEN 200
120 PRINT R$, Q$, P$, A1
140 PRINT "TYPE YØUR SEX, I.E. MALE ØR FEMALE"
145 PRINT "AND YØUR AGE";
160 INPUT S$, A2
180 PRINT "YØUR SEX AND AGE ARE" S$, A2
200 END
```

RUN

```
YØUR        AGE        IS        29
TYPE YØUR SEX, I.E. MALE ØR FEMALE
AND YØUR AGE? MALE, 23
YØUR SEX AND AGE ARE MALE        23
```

The short program in Example 3 illustrates how strings and string variables can be used in a program with considerable flexibility. Of course, strings cannot be added, multiplied, or divided and therefore should not be mixed in with algebraic formulas.

Note that the order of the variables and data read in on lines 60 and 80 is different from that printed according to line 120; the PRINT statement in line 120 will cause the computer to print our YØUR AGE IS 29. Line 140 provides direction to the person using the program about what data to enter in response to the INPUT statement in line 160: The terminal prints out TYPE YØUR SEX, I.E. MALE ØR FEMALE AND YØUR AGE? The user in this case responded MALE, 23. See Figure 10-1.

SPECIAL CHARACTER–STRING USES

In order to analyze in more detail the character-string peculiarities and capabilities, the following sections are added.

Strings with Matrices

Any list or matrix requirement can be formed by the variable name followed by the $ and subscripted alphabetics that indicate the position of each element. For example, A$ (M,N) is a string with a matrix.

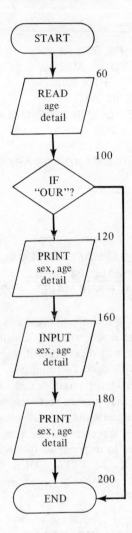

Figure 10-1.

Relational Operators

We earlier showed that string variables can be made equivalent to a constant. Now it can be shown that a string can be made equivalent also to another string variable (e.g., A\$ = B\$). Also, other operators can be used to indicate alphabetic sequence. For example, B\$ > A\$ indicates that the string B\$ occurs after A\$ in alphabetic sequence.

ASCII Conversions

Individual characters in a string can be referenced (in some computers) by using a CHANGE statement. This statement permits the user to convert a character string into a list of numeric values or vice-versa. Each character in this situation is converted to its ASCII equivalent or vice versa. ASCII (American Standard Code for Information Exchange) is a popular code in data communications. See the appropriate language manual for details of these conversions, and note Example 4.

Example 4

```
10 DIM A (20)
20 B$ = "SUM"
30 CHANGE B$ TØ A
```

String Input

The READ statement can be used to input the string variables very similar to what we have done with other variables. For example, consider

```
10 READ A$
20 DATA 100
```

This would indicate that 100 will be outputted. The quotes may not be necessary in this situation, although quite commonly used. Another example could be the output of names or dates, as in Example 5.

Example 5

```
10 READ N$
20 DATA "SMITH" or

10 READ D$
20 DATA "FEB $"
```

The INPUT statement can also be used to input strings as if they were numeric values. For example,

```
10 READ N$
20 INPUT N$
```

would do the same thing in effect as

10 INPUT "NAME"; N$

Some versions of BASIC, such as BASIC PLUS, use an effective device called the INPUT LINE statement. This allows acceptance of input lines with many types of imbedded characters such as spaces, quotes, or types of punctuation. The complete line of the INPUT statement is read as a unit.

String Functions

Many new versions of BASIC allow the use of character strings with various mathematical functions. Such functions aid in manipulating characters within a string and in using special statements such as the INPUT LINE just mentioned. An example of this would be

10 PRINT LEN (A$)

The function (LEN) in this case gives the length of the string in characters.

Summary of Rules for Strings

1. Do not use the special characters @, ?, ', ", etc. within a string without first consulting the particular dialect you are using. The apostrophe, for example, cannot be used within a string if it is used to enclose it.
2. Be careful of the number of blank spaces in a string, since they are difficult to count. Some have suggested underlining each blank for clarity.
3. Make certain all characters that are meant to be included in the string are in effect within the quotes.
4. Practically all systems use a single variable plus the $ sign. Some allow two-character numeric variable names.
5. Consult your computer manual to determine the maximum number of characters allowed in the string.

EXERCISES

1. What will the computer print out in response to the following program?

```
10 LET K = 15.9
20 LET T$ = "K"
30 PRINT K
40 PRINT T$
50 END
```

2. What two kinds of variables are there in BASIC? Give at least three examples of each type.

3. Each of the following represents a BASIC string or string variable. Debug each.
   a. ENTER ALL THE CHARACTERS IN THE STRING
   b. C
   c. C#3

4. Assign the string FEBRUARY 1979 to the variable M$.

5. Assign the string ***ERRØR*** to variables P$ and S$.

6. Enter numeric values for X1, X2, X3 and string variable X$. All of the data are to be typed on one line of a typewriter terminal.

7. Print the values of X$ and X next to each other, followed by the value of the formula $A \uparrow 2 + B \uparrow 2$

8. What is the output for

   `10 PRINT "NAME", N$, (X+Y)↑2,X`

   if the name is JØE, X is 27, Y is 5, and X is 10 to the 3rd power?

11

SUBROUTINES AND SPECIAL FEATURES

A subroutine is used when a particular part of a program is to be repeated several times at different locations within a program. It thus eliminates the need to repeat a series of statements that will be used a number of times by the program. It also finds use for complicated mathematical operations and large-volume I/O actions. Any development of a library would require extensive use of subroutines.

GØSUB STATEMENT

In timesharing, the subroutine is read into the computer along with the main program, but two special keywords are used. The keyword GØSUB, followed by the number of the first line of the subroutine, is used whenever the subroutine is to be entered by the main program. The RETURN keyword is typed as the last statement of the subroutine; it directs the system back to the line following the GØSUB line in the main program. The two keywords in the program thus might appear in the program statements as follows:

50 GØSUB
. . . .
290 RETURN

The program in Example 1 calculates the rate of return for industrial bonds on the basis of the latest bond prices and the respective coupon rates. Although this could be done without a subroutine, one has been inserted for illustration purposes. The use of a subroutine certainly simplifies the program and the task of the programmer.

Example 1

```
10 PRINT "CØRPØRATIØN", "RATE ØF RETURN"
20 READ C$
30 DATA BENDIX
35 READ P,E
40 DATA 76.5, 8.0
50 GØSUB 160
60 READ C$
70 DATA FØRD
80 READ P,E
90 DATA 47.5, 4.5
100 GØSUB 160
110 READ C$
120 DATA SEARS
130 READ P,E
140 DATA 65, 5.6
150 GØSUB 160
155 GØ TØ 190
160 LET R = (E*100)/P
170 PRINT C$, R
180 RETURN
190 END
```

RUN

CØRPØRATIØN	RATE ØF RETURN
BENDIX	10.4575
FØRD	9.47368
SEARS	8.61538

The program in Example 1 first prints out the headings for the corporation-name and rate-of-return columns. The system then reads the first corporation's name into a string variable (C$). It then reads the two numeric variables P and E and, at line 50, is directed to the subroutine which starts at line 160 and ends at line 180. Line 180 returns it to line 60, the line following the line that sent it to the subroutine. It then twice repeats what it did before, being sent to the subroutine by lines 100 and 150. Following the last subroutine exit, the system is sent to the END statement which completes the program. The flowchart in Figure 11-1 depicts the relationship between the main program and the subroutine.

In complex programs, a subroutine may be "nested" inside another. However, it is important that the nested subroutine be entirely within the other. Of course, several subroutines may be used independently of each other, as illustrated graphically in Figure 11-2.

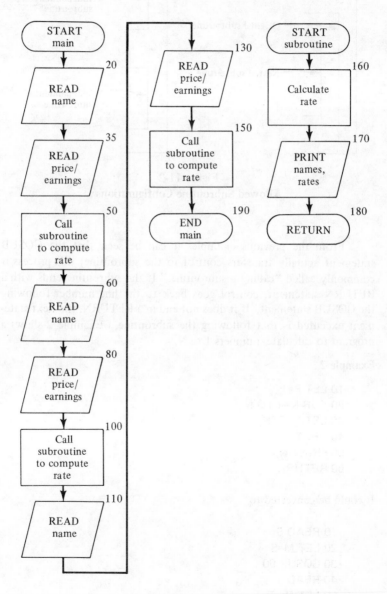

Figure 11-1

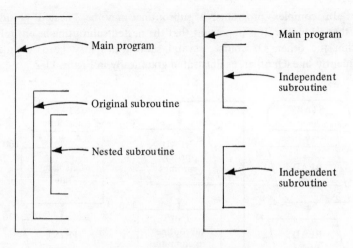

Figure 11-2
Allowed Subroutine Configurations

From the previous examples it can be seen that the GØSUB statement actually transfers control to the subroutine; this process is commonly called "calling a subroutine." If the subroutine ends with a RETURN statement, control goes back to the line number following the GØSUB statement. If it does not end in a RETURN, the next statement executed is that following the subroutine. Example 2 shows a program to calculate numbers 1 to N.

Example 2

```
10 LET P=1
20 FØR K=1 TØ N
30 LET P= P*K
40 NEXT K
50 PRINT N,P
60 RETURN
```

It could be converted to

```
10 READ S
20 LET M=S
30 GØSUB 90
40 READ T
50 LET N= T
60 GØSUB 90
```

```
70 STØP
80 LET P= 1
90 FØR K=1 TØ N
100 LET P = P*K
110 NEXT K
120 PRINT N,P
130 RETURN
140 DATA 5,10
150 END
```

Rules for Subroutines

1. When more than one subroutine is used in the same program, place one after the other in line number sequence at the end of the program.
2. If possible, use distinctive line numbers for the subroutines. For example, use higher numbers than the main program.
3. Always exit a subroutine with a RETURN statement.
4. A subroutine can call another subroutine, even itself.
5. Subroutines can be entered at any point, can have more than one RETURN statement, and multiple entry points.
6. If necessary, prepare a separate flowchart for the subroutine, so that the logic will be clear.
7. Remember that nested subroutines must have a strict hierarchical ordering. If subroutine A, for example, references subroutine B, the B cannot reference A.

SPECIAL FEATURES

Replacing Variables or Constants with an Expression

The BASIC language is quite flexible. Very often, the simple statements discussed so far can be combined or expanded to eliminate programming steps and thus shorten the program required to perform a specific task. One commonly used method of reducing the number of steps in a program is to follow the PRINT statement with a complex expression rather than just a variable. Examples 3 and 4 illustrate how a program with six statements can be reduced to one with four statements in this way.

Example 3

```
10 READ A1, A2, A3, A4
20 DATA 5, 6.93, 4E−5, .07
30 LET X1 = A1 + A2↑A4
40 LET X2 = A3*A4
50 PRINT X1, X2, A2
60 END

RUN

6.14512      2.8E−6      6.93
```

Example 4

```
 5 READ A1, A2, A3, A4
15 DATA 5, 6.93, 4E−5, .07
25 PRINT A1 + A2↑A4, A3*A4, A2
35 END

RUN

6.14512      2.8E−6      6.93
```

Note that the two LET statements in Example 3 (lines 30 and 40) are included directly in the PRINT statement of Example 4. In other words, the PRINT statement performs the functions of both the LET statement and the simple PRINT statement. This dual capability of the PRINT statement is especially useful in short programs, but in longer programs, where the values of X1 and X2 may be used again, it may not be as significant.

The FØR − TØ − statement is another one with dual capability. Provided with a beginning loop and the expression STEP, as in FØR X = A TØ B STEP C, additional capability is possible. Instead of using constants or variables for A, B, and C, the more advanced programmer might use more complex mathematical expressions. Again, this flexibility is best described with an illustration. Examples 5 and 6 show the two ways a programmer might write a short loop program.

Example 5

```
10 READ B1, B2, B3
20 DATA 5, 2, 9
30 LET X1 = B1 − B2
40 LET Z2 = B1↑B2 − B3 + B1
50 LET Y1 = B3 − B1
```

```
60 FØR X = X1 TØ Z2 STEP Y1
70 PRINT "THE X−VALUE IS" X
80 NEXT X
90 END

RUN

THE X−VALUE IS 3
THE X−VALUE IS 7
THE X−VALUE IS 11
THE X−VALUE IS 15
THE X−VALUE IS 19
```

Example 6

```
 5 READ B1, B2, B3
15 DATA 5, 2, 9
25 FØR X = B1 − B2 TØ B1↑B2 − B3 + B1 STEP B3 − B1
35 PRINT "THE X VALUE IS" X
45 NEXT X
55 END

RUN

THE X−VALUE IS 3
THE X−VALUE IS 7
THE X−VALUE IS 11
THE X−VALUE IS 15
THE X−VALUE IS 19
```

In the program of Example 6, the lines defining X1, Z2, and Y1 (lines 30 to 50 in Example 5) have been combined with the FØR − TØ − statement. Note that the two examples use loops without subscripted variables; they illustrate how this may be done. Note also that a numeric variable must appear between the FØR and the equal sign in the FØR − TØ − statement. The reason for this is rather obvious: the variable in that location is the index that changes with each cycle through the loop.

Another important group of statements in which a constant or variable can be replaced with a complex mathematical expression is the mathematical functions. Again this flexibility is especially helpful in short programs, as illustrated by Examples 7 and 8, which give the same results.

Example 7

```
10 READ C1, C2, C3
20 DATA 9, 16, 100
30 LET X1 = C1 + C2
40 LET X2 = C3/(C1 + C2)
50 LET Y1 = SQR (X1)
60 LET Y2 = ABS (X2)
70 LET Y3 = INT (C1)
80 LET Y4 = EXP (C2)
90 LET Y5 = LØG (C3)
100 PRINT Y1, Y2
110 PRINT Y3, Y4, Y5
120 END
```

RUN

```
5       4
9       8.88611E+6      4.60517
```

Example 8

```
 5 READ C1, C2, C3
15 DATA 9, 16, 100
25 LET Y1 = SQR (C1 + C2)
35 LET Y2 = ABS (C3/(C1 + C2))
45 PRINT Y1, Y2
55 PRINT INT (C1), EXP (C2), LØG (C3)
65 END
```

RUN

```
5       4
9       8.88611E+6      4.60517
```

Note that Example 8 does not contain all the possible combinations of statements. For instance, statements 25 and 35 could be incorporated into statement 45 by rewriting it as

```
45 PRINT SQR(C1+C2), ABS(C3/(C1+C2))
```

In any case, only a few of the mathematical functions have been illustrated. The same degree of complexity (or is it simplicity?) is of course feasible for all of them.

EXERCISES

1. The following portions of BASIC programs contain errors. See if you can identify them.

```
40 GØSUB 160
   . . .
160 LET C = C1+C2+C3
   . . .
190 GØ TØ 60
   . . .
220 RETURN
230 FNEND
240 END
```
Subroutine

2. Correct the following:

```
30 GØSUB 100
   . . .
100 REM SUBROUTINE X
   . . .
120 GØSUB 200
   . . .
160 RETURN
200 REM SUBRØUTINE B
   . . .
230 GØSUB 100
   . . .
250 RETURN
260 END
```
Subroutine

Subroutine

3. Write a program using a subroutine to calculate the highest dividend rate as a percentage of stock price for several common stocks.

4. Simplify the following program:

```
10 READ A, B, C, D
20 DATA 5, 7, 9, 11
30 LET X = A + B − C
40 LET Y = D/(A + B)
50 LET Z = B ↑ A − C + D
60 PRINT X, Y, Z
```

```
70 LET S = X + Y + 2
80 PRINT S
90 END
```

5.   Change the program in Example 7 to a program which uses the INPUT statement as a means of entering data.

6.   Write an interactive program which calculates the ratio of your weight (in pounds) to your length (in inches) and informs you that you are overweight if the ratio exceeds 2.5, but that your weight is satisfactory if the ratio is less than or equal to 2.5.

7.   Show how Example 1 can be simplified by combining READ statements and DATA statements.

8.   Write an interactive program which calculates your hourly salary from your monthly salary on the basis of the number of hours worked per week.

12 PROGRAMMING WITH DATA FILES

Files are used to store information in an orderly fashion. As was stated earlier, the computer has the ability to memorize, and files are one way of utilizing this amazing ability. However, any computer's memory has limited capacity. To prevent it from becoming overloaded, the computer's memory can be transferred to magnetic tape similar to that used on a tape recorder. Alternatively, a computer memory may make use of discs to store overloads of information. Discs are analogous, if not similar, to the records played on a stereo.

Although we have so far not dealt directly with data files, we have used files for storing computer programs whenever we used the command SAVE. Conceptually, the same type of file will be used in the programming with data files to be discussed in this chapter. In previous chapters we used files for storing our own computer programs; in this chapter we shall use files to store numeric and alphanumeric data for subsequent manipulation by our own programs.

COMMON FILE—HANDLING STATEMENTS

Words used in file handling would include, in many systems, the following:

1. FILES — A file-manipulation word used in a statement to inform the computer we will use a particular file name.
2. READ#, WRITE# — Words used to read and write binary files, respectively. Information, by being stored in binary form, can be read faster. Such files are called "random access."
3. INPUT#, PRINT# — Words used similarly to READ# and WRITE#, but designed for sequential teletypewriter files.
4. SCRATCH — A word used to erase all of a previous program.
5. RESTORE (RESET) — Statements, used in place of each other, to enable the computer to read a file more than once. It restores the situation in the specified file to what it was.

105

6. IF END# — A statement used to avoid the error message produced when the computer reaches the end-of-file.

See Appendix B for the systems that use the above file-handling keywords and for a more complete listing. See p. 114 for BASIC-PLUS.

Mention has been made of the READ-WRITE combination as opposed to the INPUT-PRINT. On a teletypewriter file, the information is stored in BCD, Binary Coded Decimal, and the characters are printed as if you had typed them on the teletypewriter. This type of file is sequential, since in order to obtain the 10th number stored on the file, you have to have the first nine numbers read in. A typical program for writing on a file ·with this method is shown in Example 1.

Example 1

```
10 FILES S
20 PRINT "NUMBER, SAL1, SAL2"
30 INPUT N,S1,S2
40 PRINT #1N, S1, S2
50 IF N > 10 THEN 30
60 PRINT "THANK YØU"
70 END
```

The second method, using a binary file, is faster and will be discussed in detail in this chapter. And it is random access, not requiring you to read all the preceding items on the file.

FILE PREPARATION

A data file may be prepared in various ways. It may be prepared by a computer program with internally generated data or with data obtained from other files; it may also be prepared by simply typing in the data from the teletypewriter terminal. This latter type of file preparation is the simpler and will be discussed first.

Example 2 illustrates how a numeric data file is entered into the computer's memory. To facilitate comprehension, the complete interaction with the computer is also illustrated. The underlined items comprise the input by the teletypewriter operator; the nonunderlined portions are computer responses.

Example 2

```
ØLD ØR NEW--NEW
ENTER FILE NAME--INVENT
```

```
READY
10 55, 39, 47, 86, 92,
20 11, 42, 15, 37, 56,
30 149, 506, 481, 567,
40 .89, .91, .46, .79
SAVE
READY
```

Note that the data file illustrated in Example 2, which we have named INVENT, lists eighteen data items on four lines (the data could, of course, be listed differently). Each line is identified by a line number identical to the line or statement numbers used in ordinary computer programs. Each item of data is followed by a comma. The command SAVE at the end of the list instructs the computer to keep the data in the computer memory. If, at a later time, the file INVENT is requested in a program, the computer will list out the file in exactly the form shown in Example 2.

The same procedure is used when alphanumeric data is to be stored. Suppose that payroll information must be stored, and it is to be recalled each time the payroll is prepared. The payroll information contains the employee's name, age, social security number, job status and number of dependents. Example 3 illustrates a data file that would store all of the information. Note again that each data item is followed by a comma. Commas following the last data item on a line are optional.

Example 3

```
10 GREEN J.,29,352194766,LAB,2
20 SAEL P.T.,36,274868971,CLERK,1
30 FRØAT L.,47,245782711,TECHN,2
40 CLAES T.,38,264974112,LAB,3
50 FRØST F.,41,222124209,CLERK,2
```

USING FILES IN A PROGRAM*

The worth of a numeric or alphanumeric data file is proportional to its use; the more frequently it is used, the more valuable it is. But before a file can be used in a computer program, it must be specified within the program. This can be accomplished by placing a FILES

---

*Applicable to General Electric MARK II and similar systems.

statement at the beginning of the program. Up to eight data files may be used in a single computer program, and each file name must be listed after the command FILES. For instance, if the three files INVENT, GØØD and BADLY were to be used in a program, the following statement would have to appear at the beginning of the program:

    10 FILES INVENT;GØØD;BADLY

Note that semicolons separate the file names.

FILE DESIGNATOR

Once a file has been placed in the computer memory, the user must be able to recall its data — for performing operations or whatever. He does this by instructing the computer to read the file, referring to it by its position in the FILES statement. For instance, suppose the FILES statement were:

    10 FILES HIGH;MEDIUM;LØW

Then the file called HIGH is file #1, the file called MEDIUM is file #2, and the file identified as LØW is file #3. The symbol # must always precede the file number when a file is to be read.

The most straightforward way to illustrate how data files can be manipulated is by example. In Example 4 the data file MEDIUM, with the three data items 516, 487, and 986, is entered into the computer memory. In Example 5 the file MEDIUM is read and its individual data are given the names A, B and C in line 20. Note that the READ command (line 20) directs the system to read file #2, and MEDIUM is the second file listed in the FILES statement (line 10). Line 30 then instructs the system to print out items B and C.

Example 4
    NEW FILE NAME––MEDIUM
    READY
    10 516,487,986
    SAVE
    READY

Example 5
    10 FILES HIGH;MEDIUM;LØW
    20 READ#2,A,B,C

```
30 PRINT B,C
40 END

RUN

487        986
```

Once file space has been designated and saved in the computer's memory, it can be used for storing any information. Frequently, though, the stored data is no longer needed, or alternatively the file space is needed for storing other data. Then, one can clear a file of data by use of the statement SCRATCH, followed by the file number, as in line 80 of Example 6. Use of the SCRATCH statement ensures that the file is completely emptied out and ready for other storage purposes.

Information may be entered into a file by typing it out directly as in Example 2; it may also be entered by the computer, provided, of course, that the computer already has the required data in its memory or can create the data (as will be shown in Example 6). A WRITE statement must be used if the computer is to enter data into a file; the command WRITE is followed by the file number and the data to be entered.

Example 6

```
 10 FILES HØT;WARM;CØLD
 20 READ X,Y,Z
 30 DATA 5,66,789
 40 WRITE #2,X,Y,Z
 50 FØR I=1 TØ 5
 60 LET A(I)=I
 70 NEXT I
 80 SCRATCH #2
 90 FØR I=1 TØ 5
100 WRITE #2,A(I),
110 NEXT I
120 END

RUN
```

Line 40 in Example 6 is the WRITE statement; note that only file #2 (WARM) is used in the program. The values of the three numeric variables X, Y, Z (5, 66, 789) are written into the file at line 40, after the program has first read them into the computer's memory. Then at line 80 the complete file named WARM is emptied, and at line 100 the five values of the numeric variable A(I) are written into the file. These values of A(I) are generated by the computer directly. Generation of data by the computer is quite common, especially in simulation studies, which are discussed in a later chapter. Note that the program in Example 6 generates no output because no PRINT statements appear in the program. WRITE statements enter data into files but do not produce printed output.

SPECIAL FEATURES OF FILES

If a file name cannot be designated in a program because a different file is used each time the program is run, it is possible to use a dummy file identification. The dummy identification consists simply of an asterisk(*). The name of the proper file can then be entered by way of an INPUT statement each time the program is used. For instance, the FILES statement might appear as

```
10 FILES INVENT;*;BADLY
```

Any file name can be placed in the dummy position, provided it is already in the user's library. Example 7 illustrates the use of the dummy file name and how the dummy name is replaced by that of a real file.

In addition to the WRITE statement, the previously discussed INPUT statement may be used to enter information into a file. As shown in line 90 of Example 7, the file-designator symbol # and the file number must follow the command INPUT.

Example 7

```
10 FILES AAB;*;XXY
20 READ N$,P,Q,R,S,T,U
30 DATA PPQ,15,25,35,45,55,65
40 FILE #2, N$
50 SCRATCH #2
60 WRITE #2,P,Q,R
70 SCRATCH #3
80 PRINT "TYPE IN VALUES FØR X,Y, AND Z"
90 INPUT #3,X,Y,Z
100 PRINT "TYPE IN NEW FILE NAME"
110 PRINT N$
120 FILE #2, N$
```

```
130 SCRATCH #2
140 WRITE #2,S,T,U
150 PRINT "THE VALUES ØF S, T AND U ARE" S,T,U
160 END

RUN

TYPE IN VALUES FØR X,Y, AND Z
? 75,89,95
TYPE IN NEW FILE NAME
? JACK
THE VALUES ØF S,T AND U ARE  45  55  65
```

In line 10 of Example 7 three files are designated, one of which is the dummy file indicated by the symbol *. Line 20 reads in one string variable and six numeric variables. The string variable, N$, is to serve as the file name for the second file, and it is given the value PPQ in the data statement on line 30. Line 40 is a new command that assigns the name PPQ to the second file. An alternative way of assigning the name PPQ to file 2 is to bypass the READ and DATA statements and use the statement

```
40 FILE #2, "PPQ"
```

Note that in this case the name of the file must be enclosed in quotation marks.

Line 50 clears file #2, now named PPQ, with the SCRATCH command, so it is ready to take in new data. Since file PPQ was already present in the user's library, it may have contained data, but they are cleared out by line 50. Line 60 then enters new data into file #2 by writing in the values of the numeric variables P, Q, and R.

Lines 80 and 90 illustrate the use of the INPUT statement to enter data in an empty file. Lines 100, 110 and 120 illustrate how a new file named JACK is assigned to the second file location. This new file name does not replace the file PPQ; it only removes file PPQ from contact with the program, to allow another file to be used in the program. Line 130 clears the new file #2, named JACK, with the SCRATCH command, and line 140 writes new values into that file. Line 150 then prints out the values of the numeric variables S, T and U, and line 160 ends the program. The output, including the user's responses to the INPUT statements, is shown below the program.

The next example shows an alternative way of using a dummy file.

Example 8

```
10 FILES TUT; TAT
20 FILE #2, "TØT"
30 READ D,E,F
40 DATA 99,89,79
50 SCRATCH #2
60 WRITE #2, D,E,F
70 END
```

RUN

Although the two files TUT and TAT are listed in the FILES statement, the TAT file name will be used as a dummy. Line 20 changes the file named TAT to another file, named TØT. Lines 30 and 40 simply read in three data items. Line 50 then clears the TØT file, and line 60 writes the three data items, entered into the program through lines 30 and 40, into the TØT file. The result is that the complete TØT file is now file #2. Since PRINT statements do not appear in the program, there is no output.

When a file number is called by a READ, WRITE, INPUT, or SCRATCH statement, the file number may be stated directly or, alternatively, a numeric variable may be used. Example 9 illustrates this feature.

Example 9

```
10 FILES BØY;CØY;TØY
20 READ A,D$,F$,G
30 DATA 2,HIP,HØP,299
40 SCRATCH #A
50 WRITE #A,F$,G
60 READ #A,F$,G
70 PRINT F$
80 END
```

RUN

HØP

Note that the numeric variable A is assigned the value 2 in line 30. Subsequently, file #A, which is file #2, is scratched, and data are written into it at line 50. Line 60 then reads the data in file #A (file #2), and line 70 directs the system to print out the word HØP contained in the string variable F$.

The use of numeric variables for file numbers probably has limited application. However, the READ and WRITE statements have features with fairly wide application in situations like that of Example 9. If the WRITE or READ statement is used with file #0 (zero), then the computer will print or read variables from the computer memory instead of from the file memory. These features are illustrated in the next example.

Example 10

```
 5 FILES ØNE;TWØ
10 LET A=0
20 READ #A,Y,Z
30 DATA 39,49
40 WRITE #A,Y,Z
50 END

RUN

39    49
```

Line 20 in Example 10 acts only as the usual READ statement, because A = 0. However, if the value of A were changed to 1 or 2, the values of Y and Z in the respective file (ØNE or TWØ) would be read. Because A = 0, line 40 is a WRITE #0 statement; it therefore performs the same function as a PRINT statement, as can be observed in the program output.

In previous chapters it was shown that, in a PRINT statement, it is not necessary to show the solved numeric variables to be printed out. In their place one can show a complex mathematical expression. The same holds true for the WRITE statements used for entering data into files, as is illustrated in Example 11.

Example 11

```
10 FILES ØNE;TWØ
20 READ A,B,C,D
30 DATA 5,15,25,35
40 SCRATCH #2
50 WRITE #2, (A+B)/C,D*A/B
60 END

RUN
```

At line 50, the values of the two expressions will be entered into the file named TWØ.

If line numbers are not required in a data file they can be left out by using the PRINT statement instead of the WRITE statement to enter data into a file. This feature is illustrated below.

Example 12

```
10 FILES AB;CD
20 FØR I=1 to 4
30 LET B(I)=I
40 NEXT I
50 SCRATCH #1
60 PRINT #1,B(1),B(2),B(3),B(4)
70 PRINT B(1),B(2),B(3),B(4)
80 END


RUN


1   2   3   4
```

ADVANCED FILE APPROACHES

The ØPEN Statement

Some systems* utilize, to an extent, some features found useful in CØBØL, such as the ØPEN and CLØSE statements. The ØPEN associates an external file specification (such as device, file name, and protection code) with the internal I/Ø channel. A typical statement would be

```
10 ØPEN "FILE.DAT" FØR INPUT AS FILE 1
```

This statement causes a search for an existing file. If not found, the FILE NØT FØUND message is received. Another statement could be

```
20 INPUT #L,A$
```

This statement causes input to be accepted from internal channel File 1 and associated with the variable A$. The INPUT − LINE statement can

*BASIC−PLUS, Digital Equipment Corp.

be substituted to handle any characters. Finally, we may have a PRINT statement to go with the ØPEN.

```
30 ØPEN "FILE.DAT" FØR ØUTPUT AS FILE 7
40 PRINT #7 "START ØF DATA FILE"
```

The file DAT here is opened on the disk with internal channel 7.

The CLØSE Statement

The CLØSE statement terminates I/Ø between the program and a peripheral device. It can still be reopened for reading or writing.

The KILL Statement

If we wanted to remove DAT from storage, so it could no longer be opened, we could simply use

```
10 KILL "DAT"
```

The CHAIN Statement

If we wanted to segment the program into two or more separate programs, we could write

```
10 CHAIN "DAT" 30
```

This causes the program to be loaded and started at line 30.

GET and PUT

GET is a word to be used, in some systems, to replace the "ØLD" command. The PUT word writes a single record on a device, except for disk where several records can be written with one PUT statement. An example of a complete program using the above would be this one:

```
10 ØPEN "XYZ" AS FILE 1
20 ØN ERRØR GØ TØ 100
30 ØPEN "ABC" FØR ØUTPUT AS FILE 2, RECORDSIZE 512
40 FIELD #1, 100 AS A$
50 FIELD #2, 100 AS B$
60 GET #1
```

```
70 LSET B$ = A$
80 PUT #2
90 GØ TØ 60
100 CLØSE 1,2
110 END
```

In the above example, several expanded features have been introduced: (a) Recordsize creates a buffer to allocate more space (in this case 512 for disk); (b) Field 1 and 2 associate the string names #1 and #2 with this buffer; and (c) LSET makes it possible to store values in these strings without moving them from the buffer. The program basically moves data from a file named XYZ to a device ABC (specific codes are available for the device), buffers are initialized to 512, Field statements assign A$ and B$ to these buffers, and data read at the GET #1 statement are transferred to the device buffer by the LSET statement. The PUT statement outputs the data to the device, and the program is then closed out.

It can be seen that with this file-manipulating system many new opportunities are available for business applications.

EXERCISES

1. Prepare a numeric data file to store the sex, age, weight, and height of individuals identified by a numeric variable. Identify sex by a (0,1) identification, that is, let 0 mean male, and 1 mean female.

2. Prepare an alphanumeric file to store the sex, age, weight, and height of individuals identified by their actual names.

3. Using the file constructed in Exercise 1 or 2, write a program which reads the file, extracts the ages of all individuals in that file, calculates their average age and prints it out.

4. After the program of Exercise 3 has performed its function, has there been a change in the data file?

5. Write a program which extracts from a file named BILL (shown below) the second, third and fourth data items in each line and writes them in a new file named JET.

10	17,	21,	235,	75
20	32,	29,	198,	73
30	78,	22,	195,	74
40	12,	23,	230,	72
50	19,	25,	220,	76
60	43,	31,	205,	70
70	71,	29,	247,	74

6. Write a program to clear out the file BILL used in Exercise 5.

7. Explain what the following program does:

```
10 FILES DØT;*
15 READ P$,Q$,A,B,C
20 DATA PØT,SØT,200,300,400
25 FILE #2,P$
30 SCRATCH #2
35 WRITE #2,A,B
40 FILE #2,Q$
45 SCRATCH #2
50 WRITE #2,B,C
55 END
```

8. You are keeping track of the daily closing prices of ten common stocks. How would you daily add the previous day's closing price to the file below? (The first entry is the stock symbol, and the second entry is the latest closing price.)

10 PAL,	15.4
20 ADL,	16.3
30 REN,	89.0
40 PPQ,	47.8
50 XØT	13.9
60 ZUN,	56.5
70 FRT,	129.3
80 BØV,	33.0
90 FLT,	25.7
100 GRT,	60.9

9. Write a program which will allow you to add information on more industrial bonds to a file of bond data. The data kept on

bonds consist of bond identification, coupon rate, year due and latest price. An example would be

10 ADL,7.50,1979,89.50

10. Write a program which calculates the rate of return for each bond on your list of industrial bonds in Exercise 9. Have the program print out the rates of return along with all the other data, in columns with the proper headings.

13 A SELECTION OF BUSINESS AND ECONOMICS PROBLEMS

In this chapter we shall look at a number of routine calculation and classification problems that the computer can perform very rapidly and accurately. Most of these problems are encountered in business or economic-study situations. Although the examples have been kept quite simple and short, they do illustrate the basic concepts involved. They are also complete enough so that the reader should be able to modify or expand any of them to meet his own particular computational needs.*

PAYROLL PREPARATION

In this section a simplified payroll preparation program in BASIC will be presented. The program is provided with the number of employees on the payroll, the number of hours each worked for the week for which the payroll is prepared, the tax deduction information, and the hourly rate. In our example the taxes are nil if the weekly salary is under $100, 10 percent on the salary from $100 to $150, and 20 percent on the salary over $150. Example 1 is a program that will perform the calculations.

Example 1

```
 5 REM THIS PRØGRAM CALCULATES NET SALARY AND
10 REM TAX DEDUCTIØNS
15 DIM H(200),S(200),T(200),P(200)
20 READ N' NUMBER ØF EMPLØYEES ØN PAYRØLL
25 DATA 12
30 FØR I = 1 TØ N
40 READ H(I)' H(I) IS HØURS WØRKED PER WEEK
50 LET S(I) = H(I)*4' WEEKLY GRØSS SALARY FØR EACH
60 NEXT I
70 DATA 40,41,39,16,21,44,55,60,41,42,39,32
```

*Problem chapters are appropriate to General Electric systems.

119

```
 80 PRINT "NET SALARY AND TAX IN DØLLARS"
 90 FØR I = 1 TØ N
100 IF S(I) > 100 THEN 200
110 LET T(I) = 0' TAX CALCULATIØN
120 GØ TØ 400
200 IF S(I) > 150 THEN 300
210 LET T(I) = .10*(S(I) — 100)' TAX CALUCATIØN
220 GØ TØ 400
300 LET T(I) = 5 + .20*(S(I) — 150)' TAX CALCULATIØN
400 LET P(I) = S(I) — T(I)' NET SALARY CALCULATIØN
410 PRINT P(I), T(I)
420 NEXT I
430 END
```

RUN

NET SALARY AND TAX IN DØLLARS

153	7
156.2	7.8
149.8	6.2
64	0
84	0
165.8	10.2
201	19
217	23
156.2	7.8
159.4	8.6
149.8	6.2
136	4

DEPRECIATION CALCULATION

The computer lends itself ideally to calculating depreciation charges or allowances on a proposed or actual capital investment. In the case of straight-line depreciation this may be relatively easy to do by hand. However, other depreciation formulas require extensive calculations; if they are to be done repeatedly a computer could handle them very routinely and quickly.

Example 2 is a rather simple BASIC program which calculates the annual straight-line depreciation of an investment. In Example 3 a

BASIC program is used to calculate and list the annual depreciation of an investment on the basis of both the straight-line and the sum-of-years-digits depreciation methods. The interactive INPUT statement in Example 3 allows the program to be used over and over again without alteration.

Example 2

```
10 REM THIS PRØGRAM CALCULATES STRAIGHT LINE
15 REM DEPRECIATIØN
20 REM C IS INVESTMENT TØ BE DEPRECIATED
30 REM Y IS YEARS ØF ESTIMATED LIFE
40 REM S IS SALVAGE VALUE
50 READ C,Y,S
60 DATA 50000,12,2000
70 LET A = (C − S)/Y' ANNUAL DEPRECIATIØN
80 PRINT "ANNUAL DEPRECIATIØN IS" A, "DØLLARS"
85 PRINT "FØR AN INVESTMENT"
90 PRINT "ØF" C, "DØLLARS ØVER" Y, "YEARS WITH A"
100 PRINT "SALVAGE VALUE ØF" S, "DØLLARS"
110 END


RUN


ANNUAL DEPRECIATIØN IS 4000 DØLLARS
FØR AN INVESTMENT
ØF 50000 DØLLARS ØVER 12 YEARS WITH A
SALVAGE VALUE ØF 2000 DØLLARS
```

Example 3

```
10 REM THIS PRØGRAM CØMPARES THE TWØ
20 REM DEPRECIATIØN METHØDS, STRAIGHT LINE
25 REM AND SUM ØF YEARS DIGITS
30 REM S IS SALVAGE VALUE
40 REM C IS INVESTMENT TØ BE DEPRECIATED
50 REM Y IS YEARS ØF ESTIMATED LIFE
60 PRINT "TYPE IN INVESTMENT, LIFE IN YEARS AND"
65 PRINT "SALVAGE VALUE"
70 INPUT C,Y,S
80 LET T = 0
90 FØR I = 1 TØ Y
```

```
100 LET T = T + I' SUMS SUM ØF YEARS DIGIT
110 LET A(I) = (C – S)/Y
115 REM CALCULATES STRAIGHT LINE DEPRECIATIØN
120 NEXT I
130 FØR I = 1 TØ Y
140 LET B(I) = (Y – I + 1)/T*(C – S)
145 REM CALCULATES SØD DEPRECIATIØN
150 NEXT I
160 PRINT "STRAIGHT LINE AND SUM ØF YEARS DIGIT"
170 PRINT "DEPRECIATIØN FØR AN INVESTMENT"
180 PRINT "ØF" C, "DØLLARS ØVER" Y, "YEARS WITH"
190 PRINT "SALVAGE VALUE ØF" S, "DØLLARS IS"
200 FØR I = 1 TØ Y
210 PRINT "YEAR" I, A(I), B(I)
220 NEXT I
230 END

RUN

TYPE IN INVESTMENT, LIFE IN YEARS AND
SALVAGE VALUE
? 9000, 10, 1000
STRAIGHT LINE AND SUM ØF YEARS DIGIT
DEPRECIATIØN FØR AN INVESTMENT
ØF 9000 DØLLARS ØVER 10 YEARS WITH
SALVAGE VALUE ØF 1000 DØLLARS IS
```

YEAR 1	800	1454.55
YEAR 2	800	1309.09
YEAR 3	800	1163.64
YEAR 4	800	1018.18
YEAR 5	800	872.727
YEAR 6	800	727.273
YEAR 7	800	581.818
YEAR 8	800	436.364
YEAR 9	800	290.909
YEAR 10	800	145.455

AVERAGE AND MARGINAL COST CALCULATIONS

A variety of costs are incurred in any production operation, and these costs can be identified and analyzed in a variety of ways. For instance, a manufacturing operation will incur fixed costs and a variable cost per unit produced. Given these costs in sufficient detail, along with the total number of units produced, one can derive the average and marginal costs.

Suppose a firm has incurred the cumulative production costs shown in Table 13-1. The first item in the cumulative-cost column is the fixed cost, incurred even before the first unit is produced. Subsequent items are cumulative production and total cost figures.

Table 13-1 lists only cumulative costs and quantities produced. However, it is a simple arithmetic exercise to find the marginal (incremental) and average costs for each successive unit. By subtracting the first line in the cumulative-cost column from the second line, we find that the marginal or incremental cost to produce the first is 64. Similarly, to find the marginal cost to produce the second unit, we subtract the second line from the third, and get 20. To find the average cost, we simply divide the cumulative cost by the number of units produced. For instance, for the first 3 units produced, the average cost is 357 divided by 3, or 119.

Table 13-1. Cumulative-Cost Data

Quantity produced (Q)	Cumulative cost (C)
0	258
1	322
2	342
3	357
4	370
5	383
6	402
7	433
8	482

Example 4 is a program which calculates the average cost and marginal cost for each quantity produced; the data are those of Table 13-1.

Example 4

```
10 REM THIS PRØGRAM CALCULATES AVERAGE AND
20 REM MARGINAL CØSTS
30 DIM C(100),A(100),M(100)
40 READ N
50 DATA 8
60 FØR I = 0 TØ N
```

```
70 READ C(I)
80 NEXT I
85 DATA 258,322,342,357,370,383,402,433,482
90 FØR I = 1 TØ N
100 LET A(I) = C(I)/I
110 LET M(I) = C(I) − C(I − 1)
120 NEXT I
130 PRINT "QUANTITY AVERAGE CØST"
135 PRINT "MARGINAL CØST TØTAL CØST"
140 FØR I = 1 TØ N
150 PRINT I, A(I),M(I),C(I)
160 NEXT I
170 END
```

RUN

QUANTITY	AVERAGE CØST	MARGINAL CØST	TØTAL CØST
1	322	64	322
2	171	20	342
3	119	15	357
4	92.5	13	370
5	76.6	13	383
6	67	19	402
7	61.9	31	433
8	60.3	49	482

BREAKEVEN ANALYSIS

Breakeven analysis is one of those topics which perennially seem to make life difficult for managerial-accounting students. In this section two BASIC programs which solve the breakeven problem are presented. In the first (Example 5), the breakeven point is determined on the basis of unit sales. In Example 6 the breakeven point is found in terms of dollar sales. The latter is required whenever the number of units produced is not an appropriate measure of production.

The breakeven point is that level of sales which produces neither a profit nor a loss. For a firm to make a profit, it must thus sell at a level above the breakeven point. The formula used in the calculation requires that the fixed annual cost be divided by the contribution each unit sold makes to the fixed annual cost. This contribution, in the unit-sales case, is the difference between the selling price per unit and the variable cost per unit. In the dollar-sales case it is the fraction of each sales dollar which is not required to cover variable cost. Contribution to fixed cost may also be viewed in both cases as the gross profit per unit.

Example 5

```
10 REM PRØGRAM DETERMINES BREAKEVEN PØINT
15 REM IN UNIT SALES
20 REM F IS FIXED CØST IN DØLLARS PER YEAR
30 REM V IS VARIABLE CØST IN DØLLARS PER UNIT
40 REM P IS SALES PRICE IN DØLLARS PER UNIT
50 REM B IS BREAKEVEN UNIT SALES
60 PRINT "TYPE IN F, V AND P"
70 INPUT F,V,P
80 LET B = F/(P − V)
90 PRINT "BREAKEVEN ANNUAL SALES IS" B, "UNITS"
100 END

RUN

TYPE IN F, V AND P
? 1000, 3, 5
BREAKEVEN ANNUAL SALES IS 500 UNITS
```

Example 6

```
10 REM THIS PRØGRAM DETERMINES BREAKEVEN
20 REM PØINT IN DØLLAR SALES
30 REM V IS VARIABLE CØST AS A PERCENTAGE ØF
35 REM DØLLAR SALES
40 REM F IS FIXED CØST IN DØLLARS PER YEAR
50 REM B IS BREAKEVEN SALES IN DØLLARS
60 PRINT "TYPE IN F AND V"
70 INPUT F,V
80 LET B = (100*F)/(100-V)
90 PRINT "BREAKEVEN ANNUAL DØLLAR SALES IS" B
95 PRINT "DØLLARS"
100 END

RUN
```

TYPE IN F AND V
? <u>2000, 60</u>
BREAKEVEN ANNUAL DØLLAR SALES IS 5000
DØLLARS

COMPOUND-INTEREST CALCULATION

Compound-interest problems are easily solved by computers. Example 7 is a program that calculates the amount to which P1 dollars, deposited at a periodic interest rate of R1 percent, will accumulate in each of N periods. The four columns printed out by the program show the period, the cumulative amount in dollars, the interest in dollars for the current period and the cumulative interest in dollars. The final figure printed out is the cumulative amount, consisting of the initial principal and the accumulated interest.

Example 7

```
10 REM PRØGRAM CALCULATES CØMPØUND INTEREST
20 REM N IS NUMBER ØF YEARS ØR PERIØDS
30 REM R1 IS INTEREST RATE PER PERIØD
40 REM P1 IS INITIAL PRINCIPAL
50 DIM P(50),R(50),C(50)
60 PRINT "TYPE IN N, R1 AND P1"
70 INPUT N, R1, P1
80 LET P(0) = P1
90 FØR I = 1 TØ N
100 LET P(I) = P(I − 1)* .01*R1 + P(I + 1)
110 LET R(I) = P(I) − P(I − 1)
120 LET C(I) = P(I) − P(0)
130 NEXT I
140 PRINT "AN INITIAL PRINCIPAL ØF" P1
145 PRINT "DØLLARS AT PERIØDIC INTEREST"
150 PRINT "RATE ØF" R1, "PERCENT"
160 PRINT "WILL ACCUMULATE AS SHØWN BELØW"
170 PRINT "PERIØD AMØUNT INTEREST CUM INTEREST"
180 PRINT
190 FØR I = 1 TØ N
200 PRINT I, P(I),R(I),C(I)
210 NEXT I
```

```
220 PRINT "CUM FINAL AMØUNT IS" C(N) + P1, "DØLLARS"
230 END
```

RUN

```
TYPE IN N, R1 AND P1
? 3, 10, 1000
AN INITIAL PRINCIPAL ØF 1000
DØLLARS AT A PERIØDIC INTEREST
RATE ØF 10 PERCENT
WILL ACCUMULATE AS SHØWN BELØW
PERIØD AMØUNT INTEREST CUM INTEREST
```

1	1100	100	100
2	1210	110	210
3	1331	121	331

CUM FINAL AMØUNT IS 1331 DØLLARS

EXERCISES

1. Write a program to calculate the total value of each class of inventory item listed in the file below. The columns are, from left to right, line number, item number, value in cents, and inventory class.

10	567	1065	A
20	439	945	A
30	042	2545	C
40	431	6050	B
50	134	1735	B
60	367	1400	A
70	814	1595	B
80	283	350	A
90	414	1980	C
100	906	2030	C

2. Write an interactive program which calculates the after-tax rate of return of a bond, based on the latest bond price, the coupon rate and the individual's marginal income tax rate. For instance, if someone has a 30 percent marginal tax rate and buys a 7½ percent bond at $84.50, his after-tax return is [(750 X

100)/8450](1.00 − 0.30). Note that if he buys tax-exempt bonds his marginal tax rate is essentially zero.

3.   Write a program to calculate the percentage profit for each item in the sales record listed in the file below. Have the system separate the file into, low- and high-profit items. Now suppose the fixed cost for each item is $50. Have the computer determine dollar profit for each item and print out which items are now the most profitable. The columns are line number, item number, item cost in cents, item sales price in cents, and volume of item.

10	567	149	248	563
20	893	056	109	409
30	478	427	839	219
40	321	370	819	65
50	789	495	895	108
60	674	162	329	39
70	327	238	419	42
80	148	429	949	13
90	917	318	769	148
100	728	412	959	231

4.   The present value V of a payment P to be made n years hence and discounted at an interest rate of r is: $V = P/(1+r)^n$. Write an interactive program to calculate V if P, r and n are known.

5.   If a loan of $10,000 is to be repaid at the rate of $900 per month, how long will it take to repay the loan? Interest is charged at 9 percent per year or at 0.75 percent per month on the unpaid balance. Write a program which will show the monthly payment of $900 broken down into principal and interest. What is the total interest charged during the period in which the loan is paid off?

6.   Space Peripheral, Inc. employs six sales representatives who are salaried but receive a bonus at the end of the year. The bonus is based on points each salesman accumulates monthly and the total funds available for bonus payment. Monthly bonus points in excess of 100 count double. Write a program which will calculate the bonus each salesman will receive on the basis of the monthly bonus points listed below and assuming a bonus pool of $20,000.

Sales Rep.	MØNTHLY BØNUS PØINTS											
	J	F	M	A	M	J	J	A	S	O	N	D
1	53	72	121	101	68	101	99	79	40	121	79	169
2	92	91	89	80	60	65	80	91	95	96	89	139
3	60	80	122	119	79	89	98	90	82	96	104	189
4	59	92	60	90	70	75	90	80	76	90	69	112
5	99	97	120	103	65	67	92	103	98	90	63	114
6	95	105	109	88	57	87	93	79	98	104	113	98

14 PRODUCTION-MANAGEMENT PROBLEMS

The computer has found wide acceptance in the production-management field, especially where large numbers of parts are involved, and calculations have to be made routinely to determine when and how much to order, which parts to schedule on which machines, and so forth.

ORDER POINT AND ORDER QUANTITY

The purchasing department in a production plant is responsible for those parts which are bought from outside vendors. Aside from the actual cost of the part, the purchasing man is concerned with when to place an order (the order-point problem) and the quantity to order so as to minimize costs over time (the economic-order-quantity problem). The costs we shall consider here are the holding cost and the ordering cost.

Suppose the purchasing department has N parts to keep track of. Suppose, too, that an inventory file is maintained showing, for each part, the average weekly usage rate, the order lead time in weeks, the holding cost in dollars per piece per week, the ordering cost in dollars per order, and the balance of pieces remaining. This inventory file might appear as shown in Example 1 for N = 5. In a real situation N would, of course, be much larger.

Example 1

10	15,	10,	.001 ,	50,	160
20	90,	12,	.002 ,	100,	1200
30	12,	5,	.004 ,	75,	90
40	360,	4,	.0005,	300,	1800
50	160,	9,	.0025,	480,	1650

The purchasing department is concerned with maintaining an adequate supply of inventory on hand, and so the inventory file is run through the computer once a week to record the past week's usage and to determine which parts need ordering and how much of each part to order. A computer program that would perform this function is shown in Example 2.

Example 2

```
   5 REM INVENTØRY ØRDERING PRØGRAM
  10 FILES INVENT
  20 LET N = 5' NUMBER ØF PARTS IN FILE
  30 PRINT "WHAT WAS USAGE DURING LAST WEEK"
  40 INPUT V(1), V(2), V(3), V(4), V(5)
  45 FØR I = 1 TØ N
  50 REM U = AVERAGE WEEKLY USAGE
  53 REM L= LEAD TIME IN WEEKS
  55 REM H = HØLDING CØST; S = ØRDER CØST
  58 REM B = BALANCE
  60 READ #1, U(I), L(I), H(I), S(I), B(I)
  70 LET B(I) = B(I) − V(I)
  80 IF B(I) > U(I)*L(I) THEN 120
  90 LET Q2 = 2* U(I)*S(I)/H(I)
 100 LET Q(I) = SQR (Q2) ' ECØN LØT SIZE
 110 PRINT "FØR PART" I, "ØRDER" Q(I), "UNITS"
 120 NEXT I
 125 SCRATCH #1
 130 FØR I = 1 TØ N
 140 WRITE #1, U(I), L(I), H(I), S(I), B(I)
 150 NEXT I
 160 END


RUN


WHAT WAS USAGE DURING LAST WEEK
? 15, 100, 10, 350, 170
FØR PART 1 ØRDER 1240 UNITS
FØR PART 5 ØRDER 248000 UNITS
```

Lines 30 and 40 enter the past week's usage into the computer memory (for large N it would, of course, be easier to use READ and DATA statements). Lines 50 to 120 comprise a large loop which reads the data into the file (line 60), calculates the new inventory balance (line 70), determines if an order should be placed (line 80) and, if an order is required, calculates the economic order quantity (lines 90 and

100). Line 110 then prints the part number to be ordered and the amount to order. The small loop at the end of the program (lines 130 to 150) writes the new data back into the file.

The program in Example 3 can be used to update the inventory file when previously ordered parts arrive at the production plant.

Example 3

```
    5 REM INVENTØRY UPDATE PRØGRAM
   10 FILES INVENT
   20 LET N = 5' NUMBER ØF PARTS IN FILE
   30 PRINT "ARRIVALS SINCE LAST UPDATE"
   40 PRINT "TYPE 0 FØR NØ ARRIVALS"
   50 INPUT A(1), A(2), A(3), A(4), A(5)
   60 FØR I = 1 TØ N
   70 READ #1, U(I), L(I), H(I), S(I), B(I)
   80 LET B(I) = B(I) + A(I)
   90 NEXT I
  100 SCRATCH #1
  110 FØR I = 1 TØN
  120 WRITE #1, U(I), L(I), H(I), S(I), B(I)
  130 NEXT I
  140 END

RUN

ARRIVALS SINCE LAST UPDATE
TYPE 0 FØR NØ ARRIVALS
? 0, 1200, 0, 0, 75
```

RATIO SCHEDULING

In production operations in which many batches of parts pass through a large number of machines, it is often quite a problem to determine which batch should be processed first. One relatively simple method of determining the best processing order is called ratio scheduling. Under this plan the batch that requires the most work (in the least time) is processed first.

To use ratio scheduling, one forms the ratio of the time remaining until the batch is due to the time required for the work still to be done. For instance, suppose that one batch still needs ten operations which are expected to take 45 days, processing time. The delivery date for that particular batch is 35 days away. Its scheduling ratio is then 35/45 or .777. Another batch still requires 30 days of processing but its due date is 40 days away; its ratio is therefore 40/30 or 1.333. The first batch is late (has a ratio less than 1), and the second batch has time to spare (has a ratio larger than 1). Hence, in ratio scheduling the batch with the lowest ratio is always processed first.

A simple ratio-scheduling system would begin with a file (call it BATCH) to store information about the batches that are in process in the shop. Example 4 is a typical BATCH file for six items; in practice it would, of course, be much larger.

Example 4

10	564,	500,	50,	40,	1.00
20	192,	450,	30,	35,	1.20
30	843,	150,	25,	30,	1.10
40	519,	50,	65,	60,	1.05
50	481,	800,	85,	90,	1.20
60	793,	650,	20,	40,	2.40

Each line contains information about one batch. The first item of information is the batch number, the second is the number of pieces in the batch, the third is the number of processing days remaining, the fourth is the number of days until the delivery date for the batch, and the last is the scheduling ratio that was calculated the last time that file was opened.

The next objective is to develop computer programs to calculate the scheduling ratio and to update the file at either fixed or irregular intervals. A program that calculates and prints the scheduling ratio is shown in Example 5. The large loop from lines 30 to 100 reads the BATCH file, calculates the scheduling ratios, checks which batches are late and prints batch numbers of late batches. The next loop, from lines 130 to 160, prints out a listing of the batches and their respective scheduling ratios and rewrites the BATCH file.

Example 5

```
 5 REM RATIØ SCHEDULING PRØGRAM
10 FILES BATCH
20 LET N = 6' BATCHES IN FILE
30 FØR I = 1 TØ N
40 READ #1, B(I), P(I), R(I), D(I), C(I)
50 REM B = BATCH NØ; P = PIECES; C = RATIØ
60 REM R = PRØCESS DAYS REMAINING
65 REM D = DAYS UNTIL DUE
```

```
70 LET C(I) = D(I)/R(I)
80 IF C(I) > = 1 THEN 100
90 PRINT "BATCH" C(I), "IS LATE" R(I) – D(I), "DAYS"
100 NEXT I
110 SCRATCH #1
120 PRINT "BATCH PIECES RATIØ"
130 FØR I = 1 TØ N
140 PRINT B(I), P(I), C(I)
150 WRITE #1, B(I), P(I), R(I), D(I), C(I)
160 NEXT I
170 END


RUN
```

BATCH	564 IS LATE	10 DAYS
BATCH	519 IS LATE	5 DAYS
BATCH	PIECES	RATIØ
564	500	.80
192	450	1.17
843	150	1.20
519	50	.92
481	800	1.06
793	650	2.00

The program in Example 6 updates the BATCH file for changes in days until due date (required each time a day passes) and changes owing to completion of production operations on batches. The program also prints out the numbers of those batches that are late. It does not, however, produce a detailed listing of the current status of all batches, as does the program in Example 5.

Example 6

```
5 REM RATIØ SCHEDULING UPDATE PRØGRAM
10 FILES BATCH
20 LET N = 6' BATCHES IN FILE
30 LET M = 3' DAYS SINCE LAST UPDATE
40 FØR I = 1 TØ N
50 READ S(I)' REDUCTION IN PRØCESSING DAYS
60 READ #1, B(I), P(I), R(I), D(I), C(I)
70 REM B = BATCH NØ; P = PIECES; C = RATIØ
80 REM R = PRØCESS DAYS REMAINING
85 REM D = DAYS UNTIL DUE
```

```
 90 LET D(I) = D(I) − M
100 LET R(I) = R(I) − S(I)
110 LET C(I) = D(I)/R(I)
120 IF C(I) >= 1 THEN 140
130 PRINT "BATCH" C(I), "IS" R(I) − D(I), "DAYS LATE"
140 NEXT I
150 SCRATCH #1
160 FØR I = 1 TØ N
170 WRITE #1, B(I), P(I), R(I), D(I), C(I)
180 NEXT I
190 DATA 0,1,3,2,2,0
200 END
```

RUN

| BATCH | 564 | IS | 13 | DAYS | LATE |
| BATCH | 519 | IS | 6 | DAYS | LATE |

LEARNING-CURVE CALCULATION

In a new process or production operation, the initial operating costs are usually higher than normal, because of the learning process that the operators must undergo or just because the process has to be "debugged." Considerable research has gone into the development of models to estimate these costs. A result of this research is the so-called learning-curve function

$$TC(x) = \frac{a}{1-b} \, x^{1-b}$$

$TC(x)$ is the accumulated production cost at the completion of the xth unit. The parameters a and b are determined empirically by two observations of cost, or estimates of cost at two levels of cumulative output. Experience has shown that the cost curve (or learning curve) quite accurately represents the cost behavior of production operations that are not solely machine controlled.

One can derive the average cost curve from the cumulative cost curve by dividing both sides of the formula by x. Average cost, $AC(x)$, is then

$$AC(x) = \frac{a}{1-b} \, x^{-b}$$

Suppose a firm receives an order to produce 500 pieces of a special assembly. The firm has produced a similar product in the past, and has already produced the first three pieces of the present order at a cost of $4500. It estimates that the first ten pieces will cost $10,000. With that information we can compute an estimated cost schedule for the entire batch of 500 pieces.

Given the total cost at each of two production figures, we can solve for the two parameters a and b in the total-cost formula. We simply substitute the values $x_1 = 3$, $x_2 = 10$, $TC(x_1) = 4500$, and $TC(x_2) = 10,000$ into the formulas below, which have been derived from the formula for $TC(x)$:

$$a = (1 - b)\, TC(x_1) x_1{}^{b-1}$$

$$b = 1 + \frac{\ln TC(x_1) - \ln TC(x_2)}{\ln x_2 - \ln x_1}$$

Example 7 is a computer program that calculates the parameters from the sample cost figures and lists cumulative cost and average cost for each 50th unit produced. The program contains an interactive INPUT statement to allow the user to enter the two cumulative-cost and two production figures which are used to calculate the parameters a and b according to the formulas shown above. A loop (lines 100 to 140) is then used to calculate and print out the production, cumulative cost and average cost figures for each 50th unit produced.

Example 7

```
  5 REM LEARNING CURVE PRØGRAM
 10 LET N = 500
 20 PRINT "PARAMETER CALCULATIØN FIGURES"
 30 PRINT "TWØ CUMULATIVE PRØDUCTIØN LEVELS"
 40 PRINT "TWØ CUMULATIVE CØST LEVELS"
 50 INPUT X1, X2, C1, C2
 60 LET B = 1 − (LØG(C1) − LØG(C2))/(LØG(X1) − LØG(X2))
 70 LET A = (1 − B)*C1*X1 ↑ (B − 1)
 80 PRINT "ØUTPUT     CUM CØST     AVERAGE CØST"
 90 LET P = 50' ØUTPUT INCREMENTS
100 FØR I = 1 TØ N/P
110 LET C(I) = A/(1 − B)*(P*I)↑(1 − B)
120 LET M(I) = C(I)/(P*I)
130 PRINT P*I, C(I), M(I)
140 NEXT I
```

```
150 PRINT "PARAMETERS A AND B ARE" A, B
160 END

RUN

PARAMETER CALCULATIØN FIGURES
TWØ CUMULATIVE PRØDUCTIØN LEVELS
TWØ CUMULATIVE CØST LEVELS
? 3, 10, 4500, 10000
```

ØUTPUT	CUM CØST	AVERAGE CØST
50	28600	571.00
100	45500	455.00
150	59700	398.00
200	72700	363.50
250	85200	341.00
300	93600	312.00
350	105200	301.00
400	115300	288.50
450	123600	274.50
500	132400	264.50

```
PARAMETERS A AND B ARE  .337  1430
```

There is an alternative and somewhat simpler method of calculating cost schedules for production runs subject to the learning curve. No algebraic formulas are required, and yet the computed average decreases as it does when the formulas are used. This method is called "the α percent learning curve," where α is a percentage, usually between 75 and 100. The lower the value α, the more learning (or cost reduction) is expected to take place; at an α of 100, no learning is expected at all.

The most commonly used α is 80, which gives rise to the 80 percent learning curve often encountered in the production of aircraft. Suppose a manufacturer begins producing a new type of airplane. If the first one costs $10 million to produce, and if the 80 percent curve applies, then the average cost per unit of the first two aircraft will be 80 percent of $10 million, or $8 million. Hence the second aircraft will cost only $6 million to build. If production is doubled from two to four aircraft, then the average cost per unit for the first four units will be 80 percent of $8 million, or $6.4 million. If production is again doubled to eight units, the average cost per unit for the first eight units will amount to 80 percent of $6.4 million, or $5.12 million, and so on. One disadvantage of the method is the lack of cost information at most output levels. In practice, charts are used to estimate the cost at a specified output level.

Example 8 is a computer program that calculates costs based on the α percent learning curve, assuming that the cost of the first unit or the first several units is known. Three INPUT statements enter the α percentage figure, the cost of the first N units and N itself. In the example they are, respectively, 80, 900, and 3. Hence, the average cost for the first three units is $300, that for the first six units is $240, and so forth. The program can be set to perform the required calculations up to a specified maximum output (1000 in this case). The balance of the program is self-explanatory.

Example 8

```
10 REM ALPHA LEARNING CURVE PRØGRAM
20 PRINT "WHAT IS ALPHA"
30 INPUT A1
40 PRINT "CØST ØF FIRST N UNITS"
50 INPUT C1
60 PRINT "WHAT IS N"
70 INPUT N
80 LET C3 = C1/N' AVERAGE CØST FØR FIRST N UNITS
90 LET T3 = N*C3' TØTAL CØST ØF N UNITS
100 LET C2 = C3
110 PRINT "CUM UNITS    AVERAGE CØST    TØTAL CØST"
120 PRINT N, C3, T3
130 LET M = N
140 LET C3 = A1*C2/100
150 IF N <= 1000 THEN 90
160 PRINT "END ØF PRØGRAM"
170 END
```

RUN

```
WHAT IS ALPHA
?80
CØST ØF FIRST N UNITS
? 900
WHAT IS N
?3
```

CUM UNITS	AVERAGE CØST	TØTAL CØST
3	300	900
6	240	1440
12	192	2304
24	153.60	3685
48	122.88	5885

96	98.30	9455
192	78.64	15100
384	62.91	24150
768	50.33	38650

END ØF PRØGRAM

EXERCISES

1. Write a program which finds the economic order quantities for the following parts:

Part	Current inventory	Weekly usage	Order cost	Holding cost	Lead time in weeks
A	1000	160	50	.0001	5
B	3000	570	100	.0015	4
C	25000	1800	40	.0075	10
D	8000	475	10	.0005	14
E	1475	175	50	.005	8

2. Write a program which determines when to order each part, and how many to order on the basis of economic order quantity, using the data in Exercise 1.

3. The first unit of an order for 32 units costs $1000 to produce. Compute a schedule showing the cumulative cost and average cost for all 32 assemblies, assuming the 90 percent learning curve applies. Write a program to calculate the cost-function parameters.

15

RANDOM NUMBERS AND SIMULATION

The computer's ability to perform calculations at very high speeds makes it extremely valuable as a tool to imitate or "simulate" processes from real life. Simulation is, in a sense, like building a model or "mock-up" of a situation. Automobile and aircraft firms use mock-ups of proposed new products to study their behavior under various conditions. Similarly, before a plant is built, scaled-down models of the plant and machinery are used to plan its layout and evaluate its efficiency.

A simulation study performs the same function as the model, except that instead of representing a physical phenomenon it usually represents an operational phenomenon, a process, or a series of situations such as the operation of a firm, the flight of an airplane, or the playing of a game.

Simulation studies often require the generation of random numbers. Randomly generated numbers can be used to represent chance events, and chance events occurring simultaneously or sequentially produce the situations, real or artificial, mentioned above.

RANDOM-NUMBER GENERATION

A random number generated in BASIC is really a pseudo-random number. That is, when the programmer uses the function RND a number between, but not including, zero and one is randomly selected by the computer. Or, in probabilistic terms, the function RND randomly selects a value of the random variable which is uniformly distributed between, but not including, zero and one. Every number in that range has the same chance of being selected.

Given the statement

LET X = RND

141

the system will set the numeric variable X equal to a randomly selected value between zero and one. If it is desired that X be set equal to a random number between, but not including, zero and ten, then the statement

LET X = 10*RND

is used. Similarly, if a random value between −15 and +15 were desired, then the statement

LET X = 30*RND − 15

would be used.

In all the above examples, the random number generated would be a decimal. Suppose, however, that we want the computer to generate randomly an integer between, and including one and ten. If we used the INT(X) function, in the statement

LET X = INT (10*RND)

we would end up with one of the ten integers from zero to nine, inclusive. To prevent this, we would use the statement

LET X = INT (10*RND + 1.0)

Now one of the ten integers from one to ten will be randomly selected.

THE RANDOMIZE STATEMENT

If a random number or a series of random numbers is generated with the RND statement, the same number or series of numbers will appear each time the RND statement is called. This feature is quite useful for debugging or testing programs, but it is not desirable when running actual simulations. To introduce complete randomness, the RANDØMIZE or RANDØM statement is used. This statement augments the RND statement by causing it to produce different sets of random numbers each time it is used. The RANDØMIZE statement is inserted at the beginning of the program and appears as

10 RANDØMIZE

or

        10 RANDØM

As was noted before, the RANDØMIZE statement is removed during the testing phase to ensure that any errors are found and corrected.

SIMULATION OF SIMPLE PROCESSES

The two simple processes we shall simulate are coin-tossing and die-rolling. If a coin is perfectly balanced, then the probability of tossing a head is equal to the probability of tossing a tail. Hence, to simulate a coin-tossing game, we simply assign half the random numbers that can be generated to tails, and the other half to heads. Lines 50 to 80 in Example 1 do just that.

Example 1

```
    5 REM CØIN TØSSING SIMULATIØN
   10 PRINT "TYPE THE NUMBER ØF CØINS TØ BE TØSSED"
   20 INPUT N
   25 RANDØM
   30 FØR I = 1 TØ N
   40 LET X = RND
   50 IF X < 0.5 THEN 80
   60 PRINT "TØSS" I, "IS HEAD"
   70 GØ TØ 90
   80 PRINT "TØSS" I, "IS TAIL"
   90 NEXT I
  100 END

RUN

TYPE THE NUMBER ØF CØINS TØ BE TØSSED
? 5
TØSS 1 IS TAIL
TØSS 2 IS HEAD
TØSS 3 IS HEAD
TØSS 4 IS HEAD
TØSS 5 IS TAIL
```

Rolling one die is a rather simple process. It is simulated in Example 2 and consists essentially of the generation of random integers from one to six, inclusive. The simulation of the rolling of two dice at a time is more complicated. The possible results of this experiment are the integers from two to and including twelve, but they do not appear with equal probabilities. Example 3 illustrates the two-die process.

Example 2

```
 5 REM DIE RØLLING SIMULATIØN
10 PRINT "TYPE THE NUMBER ØF TIMES DIE IS RØLLED"
15 INPUT N
20 RANDØMIZE
25 PRINT "DIE CAME UP ØN"
30 FØR I = 1 TØ N
40 LET X = INT(6*RND + 1)
50 PRINT X;
60 NEXT I
70 END

RUN

TYPE THE NUMBER ØF TIMES DIE IS RØLLED
?20
DIE CAME UP ØN
1 5 4 5 1 1 5 4 1 2 2 3 1 3 5
3 2 1 1 6
```

Example 3

```
 5 REM DØUBLE DIE RØLLING SIMULATIØN
10 PRINT "TYPE THE NUMBER ØF DØUBLE RØLLS"
15 INPUT N
20 RANDØM
25 PRINT "PØINTS ØN EACH DIE AND TØTAL"
30 FØR I = 1 TØ N
40 LET X = INT(6*RND + 1)
50 LET Y = INT(6*RND + 1)
60 LET Z = X + Y
70 PRINT X,Y,Z
80 NEXT I
90 END

RUN
```

```
TYPE THE NUMBER ØF DØUBLE RØLLS
? 3
PØINTS ØN EACH DIE AND TØTAL
5      4      9
6      2      8
1      1      2
```

JUNIOR MERCHANT'S PROBLEM SIMULATION

A junior merchant has the opportunity to go into business selling perishable widgets at a profit of $0.50 each; he purchases the widgets at $0.50 and sells them for $1.00. The right to run the business, i.e., his license, costs him $200 which he must borrow at an interest cost of $5 per period. Unfortunately, he does not know the exact demand for widgets, and any left unsold at the end of a period are a total loss. He does know, however, that demand for widgets is uniformly distributed between 10 and 30 units per period.

The junior merchant knows something about expected values and realizes that his expected gross profit is $10 per period, based on average sales of 20 units per period. However, since he has a computer available, he would like to verify that figure and simulate some higher sales periods to determine if he can increase his profit. He intends to use his profits to pay back his $200 debt and thus reduce his interest costs as quickly as possible.

Example 4 is a computer program which will allow the junior merchant to experiment with his firm.

Example 4

```
10 REM WIDGET MERCHANT SIMULATIØN
15 RANDØMIZE
20 PRINT "PERIØDS FØR SIMULATIØN TØ CØVER"
30 INPUT N
40 PRINT "TYPE PERIØDIC INVENTØRY PURCHASE"
50 INPUT I1
60 LET L(0) = 200
65 PRINT "PERIØD, GRØSS, NET, LØAN BALANCE"
70 FØR I = 1 TØ N
80 LET S(I) = INT(20*RND + 11)
90 LET G(I) = S(I)*1 − I1*.50
```

```
100 LET L(I) = L(I — 1)*1.025 — G(I)
110 LET M(I) = G(I) — .025*L(I — 1)
120 PRINT I, G(I), M(I), L(I)
130 NEXT I
140 END
```

RUN

PERIØDS FØR SIMULATIØN TØ CØVER
? <u>5</u>
TYPE PERIØDIC INVENTØRY PURCHASE
? <u>10</u>
PERIØD, GRØSS, NET, LØAN BALANCE

1	21	16	184
2	6	1.4	182.6
3	15	10.4	172.2
4	19	14.7	157.5
5	17	13.1	144.4

A QUEUING SIMULATION

An interesting simulation is that of queuing in a walk-in barber shop. Suppose the barber shop has three seats, and customers arrive at the rate of 0, 1 or 2 every five minutes. That is, if we divide time up into five-minute intervals, the probability that no customer arrives in an interval is 1/3, the probability that one customer arrives in an interval is 1/3 and the probability that two customers arrive is 1/3. Each chair serves a customer in 10 to 20 minutes; or rather the probability that a customer is taken care of in 15 minutes is 1/2, and the probability that he is served in 20 minutes is also 1/2.

Based on these specifications a computer program can be developed to provide as output, for a given period of time, waiting times, number of customers waiting, idle time, etc. The program is shown in Example 5; it is quite lengthy and self-explanatory. Initially the customers are generated by the program and then processed through the three seats, if available.

Example 5

```
 5 REM QUEUING SIMULATION
10 LET K = I = O' K=QUEUE; I=INDEX
20 LET S1 = S2 = S3 = 0' SERVICE TIMES
```

```
 30 LET C1 = C2 = C3 = 0' IDLE TIMES
 40 PRINT "QUEUE      SERVICE TIMES      IDLE TIMES"
 50 LET A = RND
 60 IF A < = .333 THEN 100
 70 IF A < = .667 THEN 95
 80 LET K = K + 1
 90 GØ TØ 100
 95 LET K = K + 2
100 IF K < = 0 THEN 500
110 IF S1 > 0 THEN 500
120 LET A = RND
130 LET K = K − 1
140 IF A < = .50 THEN 190
150 LET S1 = S1 + 15
160 GØ TØ 195
190 LET S1 = S1 + 20
195 IF S1 < = 0 THEN 205
200 LET S1 = S1 − 5
205 IF K < = 0 THEN 520
210 IF S2 >= 0 THEN 295
220 LET A = RND
230 LET K = K − 1
240 IF A < = .50 THEN 290
250 LET S2 = S2 + 15
260 GØ TØ 295
290 LET S2 = S2 + 20
295 IF S2 < = 0 THEN 305
300 LET S2 = S2 − 5
305 IF K < = 0 THEN 540
310 IF S3 > 0 THEN 395
320 LET A = RND
330 LET K = K − 1
340 IF A < = .50 THEN 390
350 LET S3 = S3 + 15
360 GØ TØ 395
390 LET S3 = S3 + 20
395 IF S3 < = 0 THEN 405
400 LET S3 = S3 − 5
405 GØ TØ 550
410 IF C1 < = 0 THEN 420
415 LET C1 = C1 − 5
420 IF C2 < = 0 THEN 430
```

```
425 LET C2 = C2 − 5
430 IF C3 < = 0 THEN 440
435 LET C3 = C3 − 5
440 GØ TØ 50
500 LET C1 = C1 + 5
510 GØ TØ 195
520 LET C2 = C2 + 5
530 GØ TØ 295
540 LET C3 = C3 + 5
550 PRINT K, S1, S2, S3, C1, C2, C3
560 LET I = I + 1
570 IF I < = 200 THEN 410
580 END
```

RUN

QUEUE	SERVICE TIMES			IDLE TIMES		
0	15	20	0	0	0	5
1	10	15	20	0	0	0

. . . .

The output of the program consists of a history of each five-minute period. The first line consists of the first five-minute period, during which time two customers entered the shop. Chair 1 was filled with a 15-minute customer; Chair 2 was filled with a 20-minute customer; and Chair 3 remained idle (hence service time for Chair 3 is zero and since there is no one waiting queue length is also zero). The service times for the three chairs are listed under "service times" and the idle times of the three chairs under "idle times." Since a chair is either in service or idle, the sum of columns 2 and 5; or columns 3 and 6; or columns 4 and 7 will always be 5 or larger because 5 is the length of the time interval.

The second line of the output consists of the second five-minute period during which time two customers entered the shop. Chairs 1 and 2 remained occupied and remaining service times were reduced by 5 minutes; Chair 3 was filled with a 20-minute customer, and one additional customer entered the queue (hence queue length is 1). Since all three chairs are occupied, the idle times listed for each chair are zero. For subsequent five-minute periods the procedures is repeated.

EXERCISES

1. Write a statement which produces a random number between −5 and +5.

2. Write a statement which produces a random number between zero and seventeen.

3. Write a statement which produces a random integer between one and seventeen.

4. Write a program to simulate the tossing of three coins at a time. Be concerned only with the number of heads (or tails) that come up at each toss.

5. Simulate the rise-or-fall performance of the stock-market average over a period of 10 market days. The market rises with a probability of 0.30 if it fell the previous day, and with probability of 0.60 if it rose the previous day. Assume that the market rose the day prior to the start of your simulation.

6. An automobile dealer's sales of new cars are distributed uniformly between zero and nine cars inclusive, daily. Write a program to simulate sales over a 20-day period.

7. (See Exercise 6.) Assume that the automobile dealer's sales are distributed according to the Poisson distribution with mean of three cars daily. Write a program to find the probability of 0, 1, 2, 3, 4, 5, 6, 7, 8, and 9 automobiles being sold daily.

8. Using the probabilities calculated in Exercise 7, simulate the automobile dealer's sales over 20 working days.

16 CORPORATE FINANCIAL MODELS

This chapter is intended as a demonstration of how a relatively limited knowledge of computer programming can be used to design and develop a rather complex corporate financial model in the BASIC language.

WHAT IS A FINANCIAL MODEL?

An important aspect of corporate planning and control activities is the projection of basic financial information into the near-term or intermediate-term future. The effective formulation of business strategy is largely dependent on management's ability to forecast the results that any strategy will have on the financial performance of the firm. Almost any financial information can be forecast into the future, but in this chapter we shall be mainly concerned with the financial accounts found on a balance sheet, income statement or cash-flow statement.

A corporate financial model is really a collection of submodels, one for each account to be forecast. Each of the submodels predicts the performance of a particular account over the specified future and the individual forecasts are then combined into an aggregate forecast.

Designing and developing a corporate financial model therefore involves a careful analysis of each account, especially in relation to other accounts and activities. Typically, the predicted levels of activity of sales, production, plant construction, etc., are used as the basis for forecasting the activity levels of other accounts. Alternatively, information may be available from which the activity levels of these other accounts can be estimated directly. However, it is not the objective of this chapter to discuss the relationhips among financial accounts; we shall here develop a model based on data for a specific firm.

Table 16-1 lists the financial data of the Clearfield Plastics Co. for 10 years. The management of Clearfield would like to be able to project these accounts from one to five years into the future. They feel quite confident about being able to predict the levels of several accounts, including sales, depreciable assets, dividends, and common stock price. However, they are not able to forecast the effects of these accounts on the balance sheet and income statement, and desire to develop a corporate financial model for this purpose.

DEVELOPMENT OF THE MODEL

Based on the stated needs of the Clearfield Co., the 10-year historical data were analyzed, hypotheses were made, regression analyses were run and the financial accounts were related as shown in Table 16-2. Production is ordinarily derived from the cost-of-sales and inventory figures for each period. However, for forecasting purposes, it was assumed that production is a known independent variable. First-period production amounted to 850 units.

Table 16-1. Ten-Year Financial Data

Account	Year									
	1963	64	65	66	67	68	69	70	71	72
Net sales	1844	2203	2697	3100	3490	3887	4527	5291	6068	6545
Cost of sales	863	940	1130	1290	1450	1490	1720	2250	2622	2797
Selling & promotion expense	739	820	1090	1200	1340	1630	1930	2090	2334	2607
Depreciation expense	42	100	71	110	120	110	90	60	76	91
Admin. expense	104	143	219	296	380	368	360	415	485	490
Misc. expense	20	40	29	40	50	70	76	79	82	86
Net before taxes	76	160	158	164	150	219	351	397	469	474
Federal taxes	32	66	72	84	65	117	189	207	247	250
Net earnings	44	94	86	80	85	102	162	190	222	224
Ret'd earnings incr.	22	71	61	52	58	68	119	140	142	119
Dividends	22	23	25	28	27	34	43	50	80	105
Current Assets	338	416	572	756	817	883	1320	1438	1862	1956
Cash	80	100	100	150	200	200	280	300	307	342
Accounts receivable	120	160	220	290	290	340	520	560	708	791
Inventory	120	140	230	300	310	320	490	540	799	766
Other receivables	18	16	22	16	17	23	30	38	48	57
Fixed assets	462	1004	878	1194	1283	1161	880	762	747	849
Current Liabilities	164	224	320	386	441	412	604	715	642	589
Accounts payable	75	105	180	230	260	240	330	390	353	344
Taxes payable	30	60	70	100	110	100	210	250	232	214
Short term debt	59	59	70	56	71	72	64	75	57	31
Long term debt	321	610	483	665	702	607	452	201	216	349
Capital stock	300	500	500	700	700	700	700	700	1025	1022
Ret'd earnings	15	86	147	199	257	325	444	584	726	845

Table 16-2. Relationships and Identities among Accounts

Relationships

Depreciation expense	$= f$ (depreciable assets)
Cost of sales	$= f$ (production, net sales)
Administration expense	$= f$ (production, net sales)
Accounts receivable	$= f$ (net sales)
Cash	$= f$ (net sales)
Selling and promotion expense	$= f$ (net sales)
Miscellaneous expense	$= f$ (production, net sales)
Federal tax	$= f$ (net before tax)
Inventory	$= f$ (production, net sales)
Other receivables	$= f$ (net sales)
Taxes payable	$= f$ (net sales)
Accounts payable	$= f$ (federal tax last year)
Long-term debt	$= f$ (depreciable assets, retained earnings)

Identities

Net before tax	$=$ net sales $-$ cost of sales $-$ depreciation expense $-$ selling and promotion expense $-$ administration expense $-$ miscellaneous expense
Net earnings	$=$ net before tax $-$ federal tax
Short-term debt	$=$ constant
Retained earnings	$=$ retained earnings in previous year $+$ net earnings $-$ dividends

Based on the relationships of Table 16-2, a computer program was developed which forecasts the financial accounts shown in Table 16-1. The program* is given in Example 1. With the 10-year data for sales, depreciable assets, common stock and dividends as inputs, the program was run and forecasts were made of the dependent variables in Table 16-2. The results, for each of the ten years for which we have data, are shown in Table 16-3. Table 16-4 is a comparison of actual and forecasted figures for the tenth year. The reader can, of course, make similar comparisons for other years with the data in Tables 16-1 and 16-3.

The purpose of the comparisons is to determine how valid the

*Since the model developed was a proprietary model, the values of the coefficients in the prediction equations have been left out of the program.

model is in making forecasts on the basis of predicted sales and predicted depreciable assets. As the reader may observe, the forecasted data are reasonably close to the actual data, and the model may therefore be declared valid. However, the main purpose of the model is to forecast for future periods, and a real test can only be made over future time. If the basic relationships among variables do not change — and in a real situation there would be significant indications of this — then the program of Example 1 can be used as a corporate financial forecasting model with considerable confidence.

Example 1

```
10 FØR I = 1 TØ 10
20 READ S(I),E(I),K(I),U(I)
25 REM SALES, ASSETS, STØCK, DIVIDENDS
30 NEXT I
35 LET N = 10
37 REM ACTUAL FIGURES FØR TENTH YEAR
40 READ S1,C1,P1,D1,A1,M1,G1,T1,N1,B1,R1,V1,H1,E1,Y1,
41 READ X1,F1,L1,Z1,K1
42 FØR I = 1 TØ N
43 READ Q(I)
44 NEXT I
50 READ A2,A3,A4,A5,A6,A7,A8,A9
51 READ B2,B3,B4,B5,B6,B7,B8,B9
52 READ C2,C3,C4,C5,C6,C7,C8,C9
53 READ D2,D3,D4,D5,D6,D7,D8
60 LET Z(0) = -7
77 LET T(0) = 25
80 LET S(0) = 700
85 LET V(0) = 100
90 FØR I = 1 TØ N
100 LET D(I) = A2 + A3*(E(I)' DEPRECIATIØN EXPENSE
110 LET C(I) = A4+A5*S(I) + A6*Q(I)' CØST ØF SALES
120 LET A(I) = A7+A8*S(I)+A9*Q(I)' ADMIN. EXPENSE
130 LET R(I) = B2+B3*S(I)' ACCØUNTS RECEIVABLE
140 LET B(I) = B4+B5*S(I)' CASH
150 LET P(I) = B6+B7*S(I)' SELLING AND PRØM EXPENSE
160 LET M(I) = C2+C3*S(I)+C4*Q(I)' MISC. EXPENSE
170 LET G(I) = S(I) - C(I) - D(I) - P(I) - A(I) - M(I)
175 REM NET BEFØRE TAX
180 LET T(I) = B8+B9*G(I)' TAX
190 LET N(I) = G(I) - T(I)' NET EARNINGS
```

```
200 LET V(I) = C5+C6*S(I)+C7*Q(I)' INVENTØRY
220 LET H(I) = C8+C9*S(I)' ØTHER RECEIVABLE
230 LET Y(I) = D2+D3*S(I)' TAXES PAYABLE
235 LET X(I) = D4+D5*T(I − 1)' ACCØUNTS PAYABLE
240 LET F(I) = 65' SHØRT TERM DEBT
245 LET Z(I) = Z(I − 1)+N(I) − C(I)' RETAINED EARNINGS
250 LET L(I) = D6+D7*E(I)+D8*Z(I)' LØNG TERM DEBT
270 NEXT I
280 PRINT "CØMPARISØN ØF TENTH YEAR DATA"
284 PRINT "VARIABLE", "ACTUAL", "PREDICTED"
285 PRINT "        ","        ","        "
288 PRINT "SALES",S1,S(10)
290 PRINT "CGS", C1,C(10)
292 PRINT "PRØM",P1,P(10)
294 PRINT "DEPR",D1,D(10)
296 PRINT "ADM",A1,A(10)
298 PRINT "MISC",M1,C(10)
300 PRINT "GRØSS", G1,G(10)
302 PRINT "TAX",T1,T(10 )
304 PRINT "NET",N1,N(10)
308 PRINT "CASH",B1,B(10)
310 PRINT "ACCT REC",R1,R(10)
312 PRINT "INV",V1,V(10)
314 PRINT "ØTHER ST REC", H1,C(10)
316 PRINT "DEPR ASSETS", E1,E(10)
318 PRINT "ACCT PAY",Y1,Y(10)
320 PRINT "TAX PAY",X1,X(10)
322 PRINT "ST DEBT",F1,F(10)
324 PRINT "ST DEBT", L1,L(10)
334 PRINT "CMN STK",K1,K(10)
336 PRINT
338 PRINT
340 PRINT
341 PRINT
342 PRINT
343 PRINT "INCØME STATEMENT"
344 PRINT
350 PRINT "SALES","CGS","PRØM","DEPR","ADM"
360 FØR I = 1 TØ N
370 PRINT S(I),C(I),P(I),D(I),A(I)
380 NEXT I
390 PRINT
```

```
400 PRINT
410 PRINT
420 PRINT "MISC", "GRØSS", "TAX", "NET"
430 FØR I = 1 TØ N
440 PRINT M(I),G(I),T(I),N(I)
450 NEXT I
460 PRINT
470 PRINT "BALANCE SHEET"
480 PRINT
490 PRINT "CASH", "ACCT REC", "INV", "ØTHER ST REC"
495 PRINT "DEPR ASSETS"
500 FØR I = 1 TØ N
510 PRINT B(I),R(I),V(I),H(I),E(I)
520 NEXT I
530 PRINT
540 PRINT
550 PRINT
560 PRINT "ACCT PAY", "TAX PAY", "ST DEBT"
565 PRINT "LT DEBT", "RET EARN"
570 FØR I = 1 TØ N
580 PRINT Y(I),X(I),F(I),L(I),Z(I)
590 NEXT I
600 PRINT
610 PRINT
620 PRINT
630 PRINT "CMN STK"
640 FØR I = 1 TØ N
650 PRINT K(I)
660 NEXT I
800 DATA 1844,462,300,22, 2203,1004,500,23,2697,878,500,
805 DATA 25,3100,1194
810 DATA 700,28,3490,1283,700,27,3887,1161,700,34,4527,
815 DATA 880,700,43
820 DATA 5291,762,700,50,6068,747,1025,80,6545,844,1022,
825 DATA 105
830 DATA 6545,2797,2607,91,490,86,474,250,224,342,791,
835 DATA 766,57,844
840 DATA 344,214,31,344,845,1022
850 DATA 850,960,1220,1360,1460,1500,1890,2300,2881,2764
999 END
```

Table 16-3. Forecasted Values for 10-Year Period

INCOME STATEMENT

SALES	CGS	PRØM	DEPR	ADM
1844	603.656	929.294	43.9076	166.468
2203	752.584	1055.12	95.506	198.248
2697	992.986	1228.27	83.5108	232.503
3100	1165.56	1369.52	113.594	266.738
3490	1320.98	1506.21	122.067	302.963
3887	1459.02	1645.36	110.452	345.228
4527	1787.82	1869.67	33.7012	384.971
5291	2162.2	2137.45	72.4676	437.26
6068	2596.49	2409.79	71.0396	476.132
6545	2708.45	2576.97	80.274	541.312

MISC	GRØSS	TAX	NET
24.6473	76.0275	28.9196	47.1079
31.7365	69.8036	25.4361	44.3675
36.8637	122.87	55.1374	67.7327
44.1181	140.474	64.9902	75.4837
52.6501	185.129	89.9835	95.1452
63.9677	262.978	133.556	129.422
68.3457	332.484	172.458	160.026
75.9389	405.684	213.428	192.256
76.6739	437.873	231.445	206.429
97.3037	540.684	288.988	251.696

BALANCE SHEET

CASH	ACCT REC	INV	ØTHER ST REC	DEPR ASSETS
81.1099	104.542	112.308	10.6295	462
102.085	157.746	148.621	13.6757	1004
130.948	230.956	235.581	17.8673	878
154.494	290.681	281.969	21.2868	1194
177.281	348.479	314.779	24.5959	1283
200.476	407.314	327.136	27.9645	1161
237.87	502.162	457.896	33.3949	880
282.508	615.887	595.072	39.8775	762
327.906	730.539	790.431	46.4704	747
355.776	801.23	749.076	50.5178	844

Table 16-3. Forecasted Values for 10-Year Period (Continued)

BALANCE SHEET (Continued)

ACCT PAY	TAX PAY	ST DEBT	LT DEBT	RET EARN
126.793	57.6217	65	295.367	18.1079
149.127	61.3139	65	607.608	39.4754
178.518	58.0325	65	520.417	82.2081
203.386	86.0111	65	691.738	129.692
227.889	95.2925	65	723.221	197.837
253.594	118.836	65	622.251	293.259
291.016	159.884	65	421.149	410.285
336.375	196.527	65	308.193	552.54
380.481	235.121	65	260.663	678.969
413.403	252.093	65	272.302	825.665

CMN STK
300
500
500
700
700
700
700
700
1025
1022

Table 16-4. Comparison of Tenth Year

VARIABLE	ACTUAL	PREDICTED
SALES	6545	6545
CGS	2797	2708.45
PRØM	2607	2576.97
DEPR	91	80.274
ADM	490	541.312
MISC	86	97.3037
GRØSS	474	540.684
TAX	250	288.988
NET	224	251.696

Table 16-4. Comparison of Tenth Year (Continued)

VARIABLE	ACTUAL	PREDICTED
CASH	342	355.776
ACCT REC	791	801.23
INV	766	749.076
ØTHER ST REC	57	50.5178
DEPR ASSETS	844	844
ACCT PAY	344	413.403
TAX PAY	214	252.093
ST DEBT	31	65
LT DEBT	344	272.802
CMN STK	1022	1022

CONCLUSION

The purpose of this chapter has been to illustrate how even a limited knowledge of programming allows one to design, develop and implement a relatively complex financial model. The reader interested in more background on corporate financial modeling is urged to read "Building a Corporate Financial Model" by George Gershefsky in Harvard Business Review, July-August 1969, pages 1-12.

17

A SELECTION OF STATISTICS PROBLEMS

In this chapter we present a variety of statistical problems programmed in the BASIC computer language. Although the reader may use these programs directly, they are presented with the intention of motivating him to do his own programs for similar or related problems.

Any problem can be programmed in a number of different ways, and the examples in this chapter are not exceptions. One very interesting and useful exercise for the beginner is to attempt to re-program each example in a more efficient way — provided, of course, that he arrives at the same solution.

SUM OF A SERIES

In this section we write several programs which determine the sum of an arithmetic series. In Example 1 we find the sum of the first N integers, where the numeric variable N can, of course, take on any integer value.

Example 1

```
10 REM THIS PRØGRAM FINDS SUM ØF FIRST N INTEGERS
20 READ N
30 DATA 10
40 LET S = 0' S STANDS FOR SUM
50 FØR I = 1 TØ N
60 LET S = S + I
70 NEXT I
80 PRINT "THE SUM ØF THE FIRST" N, "INTEGERS IS" S
90 END

RUN

THE SUM ØF THE FIRST 10 INTEGERS IS 55
```

In the next example we find the sum of the squares of the first N integers and the sum of the first N integers. We then subtract the latter sum from the former and identify the difference by the numeric variable D.

Example 2

```
10 REM THIS PRØGRAM FINDS THE DIFFERENCE
15 REM BETWEEN THE SUM ØF THE FIRST
20 REM N INTEGERS AND INTEGERS SQUARED
30 READ N
40 DATA 5
50 LET S1 = S2 = 0
60 FØR I = 1 TØ N
70 LET S1 = S1 + I
80 LET S2 = S2 + I↑2
90 NEXT I
100 LET D = S2 - S1
110 PRINT "THE DIFFERENCE ØF THE FIRST" N
115 PRINT "INTEGERS IS" D
120 END

RUN

THE DIFFERENCE ØF THE FIRST 5
INTEGERS IS 40
```

The final example in this section is a program that finds the sum of all numbers less than some integer N that are evenly divisible by 5. Thus, if N were equal to 13, the sum would consist of 5 and 10, which add up to 15.

Example 3

```
10 REM THIS PRØGRAM FINDS SUM ØF NUMBERS
20 REM DIVISIBLE BY FIVE AND FØRMING INTEGERS
30 READ N
40 DATA 46
50 LET S = 0
60 FØR I = 0 TØ N STEP 5
70 LET S = S + I
80 NEXT I
90 PRINT "THE SUM FØR N IS" N, "IS" S
```

100 END

RUN

THE SUM FØR N IS 46 IS 225

CALCULATING AVERAGES (MEANS)

The program in Example 4 calculates the average age of a number of children. It may, of course, be modified to calculate the average of any collection of data items.

Example 4

```
10 REM THIS PRØGRAM CALCULATES AVERAGE AGE
20 REM ØF A GRØUP ØF N CHILDREN
30 READ N
40 DATA 8
50 FØR I = 1 TØ N
60 READ A(I)' AGE ØF EACH CHILD
70 NEXT I
80 DATA 5,6,8,7,4,8,3,7
90 LET T = 0
100 FØR I = 1 TØ N
110 LET T = T + A(I)
120 NEXT I
130 LET M = T/N
140 PRINT "THE AVERAGE AGE ØF THE" N, "CHILDREN"
145 PRINT "IS" M, "YEARS"
150 END
```

RUN

THE AVERAGE AGE OF THE 8 CHILDREN
IS 6 YEARS

The next example is a program that calculates the average of some grouped data. In this case the data are the ages of children, grouped as 0, 1, 2, and 3-year-olds; the age groups contain 5, 7, 9, and 8 children, respectively. The program calculates the average age of the 29 children as if it were given each data item separately.

Example 5

```
10 REM PRØGRAM TØ CALCULATE AVERAGE AGE ØF
20 REM CHILDREN GRØUPED BY AGE CLASSIFICATIØN
30 READ N' NUMBER ØF AGE GRØUPINGS
40 DATA 4
50 FØR I = 1 TØ N
60 READ S(I)
65 REM NUMBER ØF CHILDREN IN EACH AGE GRØUPING
70 NEXT I
80 DATA 5,7,9,8
90 LET T = N1 = 0
100 FØR I = 1 TØ N
110 LET T = S(I) * (I−1)+T
120 LET N1 = N1 + S(I)
130 NEXT I
140 LET A = T/N1
150 PRINT "AVERAGE AGE ØF THE" N1, "CHILDREN IS"
155 PRINT A, "YEARS"
160 END

RUN

AVERAGE AGE ØF THE 29 CHILDREN IS
1.68966 YEARS
```

CALCULATING THE GEOMETRIC MEAN

The geometric mean is sometimes more appropriate than the arithmetic mean, especially for averaging index numbers, percentages, and other ratios. It is also a useful average for frequency distributions of absolute-valued data that are skewed to the right. In Example 6, a BASIC computer program is presented for calculating the geometric mean. The data items must be larger than zero, because the geometric mean is obtained by averaging the logarithms of the data items and then taking the antilogarithm of the average. The formula for the geometric mean is

$$\log G = \frac{\sum_{i=1}^{N} \log X_i}{N}$$

where G is the logarithmic mean, N is the number of data items, and the X_i's are the data items.

Example 6

```
10 REM THIS PRØGRAM FINDS GEØMETRIC MEAN
20 READ N
30 DATA 7' NUMBER ØF DATA ITEMS
40 LET S = 0' S IS THE SUM ØF LØG ØF DATA ITEMS
50 FØR I = 1 TØ N
60 READ D(I)' VALUE ØF DATA ITEM
70 NEXT I
80 DATA 10,20,60,12,18,30,50
90 FØR I = 1 TØ N
100 LET S = S + LØG (D(I))
110 NEXT I
120 LET X = S/N
125 LET G = EXP (X)
130 PRINT "THE GEØMETRIC MEAN IS" G
140 END

RUN

THE GEØMETRIC MEAN IS 35.8
```

CALCULATING THE MEDIAN

The median of any set of N data items is the middle value in order of size if N is odd, or the mean of the two middle values if N is even. Especially when there are a few very large or small values, the median may be superior to the mean as an average. The BASIC computer program in Example 7 finds the median value of a set of data. The reader should pay particular attention to the ten statements following line 80, which order the data items from the lowest to the highest.

Example 7

```
10 REM THIS PRØGRAM FINDS THE MEDIAN
15 DIM D(15)
20 READ N' NUMBER ØF DATA ITEMS
30 DATA 11
40 FØR I = 1 TØ N
```

```
50 READ D(I)' VALUE ØF EACH DATA ITEM
60 NEXT I
70 DATA 13,9,18,17,16,7,6,21,19,15,14
75 REM NEXT TEN STATEMENTS ØRDER DATA FRØM
78 REM LØW TØ HIGH
80 LET N1 = N − 1
90 FØR I = 1 TØ N1
100 LET N2 = N − 1
110 FØR J = 1 TØ N2
120 IF D(J) < = D (J+1) THEN 160
130 D1 = D(J)
140 D(J) = D(J+1)
150 D(J+1) = D1
160 NEXT J
170 NEXT I
175 REM CHECK IF N IS EVEN ØR ØDD
180 LET H = N/2
190 IF H <> INT (H) THEN 220
195 REM CALCULATE MEDIAN FØR N IS EVEN
200 LET M = (D(H) + D(H+1))/2
210 GØ TØ 240
215 REM CALCULATE MEDIAN FØR N IS ØDD
220 LET H = (N+1)/2
230 LET M = D(H)
240 PRINT "THE MEDIAN IS" M
250 END

RUN

THE MEDIAN IS 15
```

DETERMINING DEVIATIONS

Two deviations will be discussed in this section — the mean deviation and the standard deviation. The mean deviation is simply the mean of the absolute values of the deviations of all the data items from some central mean such as the arithmetic mean. Only the absolute values of the deviations have any meaning, because the sum of the actual deviations from the mean will always be zero. The formula for the mean deviation is

$$M = \frac{\sum\limits_{i=1}^{N} |X_i - \bar{X}|}{N}$$

where M is the mean deviation, N is the number of data items, $\bar{X}$ is the mean and the X_i's are the data items. The program in Example 8 finds the mean deviation of a set of data items.

Example 8

```
10 REM PRØGRAM DETERMINES MEAN DEVIATIØN
20 READ N' NUMBER OF DATA ITEMS
30 DATA 9
40 LET S = S1 = 0' SETS THE SUMMERS EQUAL TØ ZERØ
50 FØR I = 1 TØ N
60 READ D(I)
70 LET S = S + D(I)
80 NEXT I
90 DATA 9,11,14,17,7,6,10,12,13
100 LET A = S/N' CALCULATES THE MEAN
110 FØR I = 1 TØ N
120 LET S1 = S1 + ABS(D(I)−A)
130 NEXT I
140 LET M = S1/N' CALCULATES THE MEAN DEVIATIØN
150 PRINT "MEAN DEVIATIØN IS" M, "AND MEAN IS" A
160 END
```

RUN

MEAN DEVIATIØN IS 2.667 AND MEAN IS 11

The standard deviation is the square root of the variance. It is found by the formula

$$V = \left[\frac{\sum\limits_{i=1}^{N} (X_i - \bar{X})^2}{N-1} \right]^{1/2}$$

where V is the standard deviation and the other symbols are as defined above for the mean deviation. The next example is a program that calculates the standard deviation.

Example 9

```
 5 REM PRØGRAM CALCULATES STANDARD DEVIATIØN
10 DIM D(15)
20 READ N' NUMBER ØF DATA ITEMS
30 DATA 11
40 LET S = S1 = 0' SETS THE SUMMERS EQUAL TØ ZERØ
50 FØR I = 1 TØ N
60 READ D(I)
70 LET S = S + D(I)
80 NEXT I
90 DATA 9,12,14,8,7,13,15,16,6,19,13
100 LET A = S/N' CALCULATES THE MEAN
110 FØR I = 1 TØ N
120 LET S1 = S + (D(I) − A)↑2
130 NEXT I
140 LET V1 = S1/(N − 1)' CALCULATES THE VARIANCE
150 LET V = SQR(V1)' CALCULATES STANDARD DEVIATIØN
160 PRINT "STANDARD DEVIATIØN IS" V, "AND MEAN"
165 PRINT "IS" A
170 END


RUN


STANDARD DEVIATIØN IS 3.65 AND MEAN
IS 12
```

EXPECTED-VALUE CALCULATIONS

Expected-value calculations are directly related to the deviation calculations of the last section and are especially appropriate for computer-programming applications. The expected value of a discrete random variable X is defined as

$$E(X) = \sum_{i=1}^{N} X_i P(X_i)$$

where $E(X)$ is the expected value of X and $P(X_i)$ is the probability associated with a particular value X_i. Example 10 is a program that calculates $E(X)$; note (line 70) that we multiply each value of X by its probability and sum the products.

Example 10

```
10 REM THIS PRØGRAM CALCULATES EXPECTED VALUES
20 READ N
30 DATA 4
40 LET E = 0
50 FØR I = 1 TØ N
60 READ X(I), P(I)' DATA ITEMS AND RESPECTIVE
65 REM PRØBABILITIES
70 LET E = E + X(I) *P(I)
75 NEXT I
80 DATA 4,.10,6,.40,3,.30,9,.20
90 PRINT "EXPECTED VALUE IS" E
100 END
```

RUN

EXPECTED VALUE IS 5.5

The variance W of a discrete random variable X distributed according to some specified probability distribution can be found by the formula

$$W = \sum_{i=1}^{N} [X_i - E(X)]^2 P(X_i)$$

The standard deviation can be found by taking the square root of the variance. Example 11 illustrates how both the standard deviation and the variance might be calculated by a BASIC program.

Example 11

```
10 REM PRØGRAM CALCULATES THE VARIANCE AND
20 REM STANDARD DEVIATIØN ØF A DISCRETE RANDØM
25 REM VARIABLE
30 READ N
40 DATA 5
50 LET W = E = 0
60 FØR I = 1 TØ N
70 READ X(I),P(I)
80 LET E = E + X(I)*P(I)
90 NEXT I
```

```
100 FØR I = 1 TØ N
110 LET W = W + (X(I) − E)↑2*P(I)
120 NEXT I
130 DATA 5,.10,9,.15,11,.20,7,.25,14,.30
140 LET V = SQR(W)
150 PRINT "THE MEAN IS" E
160 PRINT "THE VARIANCE IS" W
170 PRINT "THE STANDARD DEVIATIØN IS" V
180 END

RUN

THE MEAN IS 10.0
THE VARIANCE IS 9.90
THE STANDARD DEVIATIØN IS 3.14
```

BINOMIAL PROBABILITIES

The formula for calculating binomial probabilities can be represented as

$$B(X;N,P) = \frac{N!}{(N - X)!X!} \, P^X(1 - P)^{N - X}$$

where $B(X;N,P)$ stands for the probability of X successes in N independent trials, with the probability of success in any one trial equal to P. Example 12 is a BASIC computer program that performs these calculations.

Example 12

```
10 REM THIS PRØGRAM FINDS BINØMIAL PRØBABILITY
20 READ X,N,P
30 DATA 2,6,.40
35 LET S1 = 1
40 FØR I = 1 TØ X
50 LET S1 = S1*I' X FACTØRIAL
60 NEXT I
70 LET S2 = 1
80 FØR I = 1 TØ N
90 LET S2 = S2*I' N FACTØRIAL
100 NEXT I
110 LET S3 = 1
```

```
120 FØR I = 1 TØ N − X
130 LET S 3 = S3*I' N − X FACTØRIAL
140 NEXT I
150 LET B = S2/(S1*S3)*P↑X*(1 − P)↑(N − X)
160 PRINT "BINØMIAL PRØBABILITY IS" B
165 PRINT "FØR B(X;N,P)"
170 PRINT "WHERE X IS" X, "N IS" N, "AND P IS" P
180 END
```

RUN

```
BINØMIAL PRØBABILITY IS .31104
FØR B(X;N,P)
WHERE X IS 2, N IS 6, AND P IS .40
```

Example 13 calculates cumulative binomial probabilities. Note that in Example 13 an interactive INPUT statement is used instead of the common READ statement; this allows the same program to be used repeatedly with different data. The cumulative binomial function can be represented as

$$F(Y;N,P) = \sum_{X=0}^{Y} \frac{N!}{(N-X)!X!} P^X(1 - P)^{N - X}$$

where $F(Y;N,P)$ is the cumulative probability of $0,1,2,...,Y$ successes in N independent trials, with the probability of success in any one trial equal to P. It follows, of course, that Y is less than or equal to N.

Example 13

```
  5 REM THIS PRØGRAM FINDS CUMULATIVE BINØMIAL
 10 REM PRØBABILITIES IN TERMS ØF F (Y) = F (Y;N,P)
 15 PRINT "PRØGRAM FINDS CUMULATIVE BINØMIAL"
 20 PRINT "PRØBABILITIES IN TERMS ØF F(Y) = F(Y;N,P)"
 30 PRINT "TYPE IN Y,N,P"
 40 INPUT Y,N,P
 50 LET F = 0
 60 LET S1 = 1
 70 FØR I = 1 TØ N
 80 LET S1 = S1*I' N FACTØRIAL
 90 NEXT I
100 FØR X = 0 TØ Y
```

```
110 LET S2 = S3 = 1
120 FØR I = 1 TØ X
130 LET S2 = S2*I' X FACTØRIAL
140 NEXT I
150 FØR I = 1 TØ N − X
160 LET S3 = S3*I' N − X FACTØRIAL
170 NEXT I
180 LET F = F + S1/(S2*S3)*P↑X*(1 − P)↑(N − X)
190 NEXT X
200 PRINT "CUMULATIVE BINØMIAL PRØBABILITY IS" F
210 PRINT "FØR F(Y;N,P) WHERE Y IS" Y
220 PRINT "N IS" N, "AND P IS" P
230 END


RUN


THIS PRØGRAM FINDS CUMULATIVE BINØMIAL
PRØBABILITIES IN TERMS ØF F(Y) = F(Y;N,P)
TYPE IN Y,N,P
?7,9,.40
CUMULATIVE BINØMIAL PRØBABILITY IS 2.12E−2
FØR F(Y;N,P) WHERE Y IS 7
N IS 9 AND P IS .40
```

POISSON PROBABILITIES

The Poisson probability distribution is presented in this section. It is also a discrete distribution, and therefore easy to work with, using a BASIC computer program.

In its general form a Poisson probability is written as

$$P(X;M) = \frac{e^{-M}M^X}{X!}$$

where $P(X;M)$ is the probability of X successes in a given interval if the average number of successes during the interval is M. Example 14 illustrates how to calculate $P(X;M)$ with a BASIC computer program. The interactive INPUT statement is used to enter data.

Example 14

```
10 REM PRØGRAM FØR PØISSØN PRØBABILITIES
20 PRINT "PRØGRAM FØR PØISSØN PRØBABILITIES"
30 PRINT "TYPE IN X AND M AFTER QUESTIØN MARK"
40 INPUT X,M
50 LET S = 1
60 FØR I = 1 TØ X
70 LET S = S*I
80 NEXT I
90 LET P = EXP(–M)*M↑X/S
100 PRINT "PØISSØN PRØBABILITY FØR X IS" X, "AND"
105 PRINT "M IS" M, "IS" P
110 END
```

```
RUN
```

```
PRØGRAM FØR PØISSØN PRØBABILITIES
TYPE IN X AND M AFTER QUESTIØN MARK
?3,5
PØISSØN PRØBABILITY FØR X IS 3 AND
M IS 5 IS 0.1404
```

In Example 15 the cumulative Poisson probability is calculated. Its mathematical formula is

$$F(Y;M) = \sum_{X=0}^{Y} \frac{e^{-M}M^X}{X!}$$

where $F(Y;M)$ is the probability of Y or fewer successes in the given interval.

Example 15

```
10 REM THIS PRØGRAM CALCULATES THE CUMULATIVE
20 REM PØISSØN PRØBABILITY F(Y) = F(Y;M)
30 PRINT "PRØGRAM CALCULATES THE CUMULATIVE"
40 PRINT "PØISSØN PRØBABILITY F(Y) = F(Y;M)"
50 PRINT "TYPE IN Y AND M AFTER QUESTIØN MARK"
```

```
60 INPUT Y,M
70 LET F = 0
80 FØR X = 0 TØ Y
90 LET S = 1
100 FØR I = 1 TØ X
110 LET S = S*I
120 NEXT I
130 LET F = F + EXP(−M)*M↑X/S
140 NEXT X
150 PRINT "CUMULATIVE PØISSØN PRØBABILITY FØR Y"
155 PRINT "IS" Y
160 PRINT "AND M IS" M, "IS" F
170 END


RUN


PRØGRAM CALCULATES THE CUMULATIVE
PØISSØN PRØBABILITY F(Y) = F(Y;M)
TYPE IN Y AND M AFTER QUESTIØN MARK
? 3,4
CUMULATIVE PØISSØN PRØBABILITY FØR Y IS 3
AND M IS 4 IS 0.43347
```

BAYESIAN PROBABILITIES

The use of Bayes' Theorem allows one to calculate posterior (after-the-fact) probabilities from prior (before-the-fact) and conditional probabilities. (The latter might be derived from an experiment or survey.)

Bayesian analysis has many practical applications but is most easily explained with the somewhat naive jar-and-colored-balls example. Suppose we have two jars, each containing black and red balls. Our experiment consists of two parts: first a jar is chosen, and then a ball is taken from that jar. We know the prior probabilities, that is, the probability that a particular jar is chosen in the first part of the experiment, and we know how many balls of each color are in each jar. Then Bayes' theorem allows us to calculate the probability that the ball that was drawn came from a particular jar (the posterior probabilities).

Suppose the probability of initially choosing jar 1 is $P(J_1)$ = .20, and that of choosing jar 2 is $P(J_2)$ = .80. Suppose also that jar 1 contains 3 black and 7 red balls, jar 2 contains 4 black and 6 red balls, and a black ball (B) was drawn. We wish to know which jar it came from. The data of the problem and some of the probabilities can be tabulated as follows:

	$P(J_i)$	$P(B\|J_i)$	$P(J_i)\,P(B\|J_i)$	$P(J_i\|B)$
Jar 1 (J_1)	.20	.30	.06	.06/.38
Jar 2 (J_2)	.80	.40	.32	.32/.38
Total	1.00		$P(B){=}.38$	1.00

The probabilities in the $P(J_i)$ and $P(B|J_i)$ columns are calculated from the data given. The joint probabilities in the third column are calculated from the two previous columns, and the posterior probabilities in the last column are found using the third-column entries and the sum of the third column, which is $P(B)$.

In mathematical form, Bayes' theorem would be stated as follows (in the notation of our example):

$$P(J_i|B) = \frac{P(B|J_i)P(J_i)}{P(B|J_1)P(J_1)+P(B|J_2)P(J_2)}$$

where $P(J_i|B)$ for i = 1 and 2 are the entries in the last column of the table. The BASIC program in Example 16 solves the problem we have been discussing.

Example 16

```
10 REM THIS PRØGRAM CALCULATES PØSTERIOR
20 REM BAYESIAN PRØBABILITIES
30 READ P1,P2' PRIØR PRØBABILITIES
40 DATA .20,.80
50 READ C1,C2' CØNDITIØNAL PRØBABILITIES
60 DATA .30,.40
70 REM CALCULATE JØINT PRØBABILITIES
80 LET J1 = P1*C1
90 LET J2 = P2*C2
100 LET M = J1 + J2' MARGINAL PRØBABILITIES
110 LET R1 = J1/M
120 LET R2 = J2/M
130 PRINT "PØST.PRØB.IS" R1, "FØR PRIØR PRØB. ØF" P1
140 PRINT "PØST.PRØB.IS" R2, "FØR PRIØR PRØB. ØF" P2
150 END
```

RUN

PØST.PRØB.IS .158 FØR PRIØR PRØB. ØF .20
PØST.PRØB.IS .842 FØR PRIØR PRØB. ØF .80

FIBONACCI NUMBERS

In the thirteenth century, Leonardo Fibonacci, a wealthy Italian merchant who was fascinated with numbers, discovered what is now known as the Fibonacci numbers or series. Each number of the Fibonacci series is the sum of the two numbers immediately preceding it. That is if n_1 and n_2 are the first two numbers, then $n_3 = n_1 + n_2$, and $n_4 = n_2 + n_3$, and so forth. The Fibonacci series thus is

$$1,1,2,3,5,8,13,21,34,55,89,144,233,377,610,987,...$$

Fibonacci numbers have many interesting properties. One is that the square of any number in the series, and the product of the numbers immediately before and after it, always differ by 1. For instance, $8^2 = 5 \times 13 - 1$ and $13^2 = 8 \times 21 + 1$. Also note that the series consists of two odd numbers followed by an even number, two more odd numbers followed by an even number, etc.

Example 17 is a program which computes the first five Fibonacci numbers, their respective squares and the product of the numbers immediately before and after each of them. Lines 70 to 120 compute the Fibonacci series and the squares of the numbers in the series. Lines 130 to 160 calculate the product of the numbers before and after each number in the series, and lines 170 to 190 print out the numbers, squares and products.

Example 17

```
10 REM FIBØNACCI SERIES GENERATØR
20 DIM N(25), P(25), S(25)
30 PRINT "LIST ØF FIBØNACCI NUMBERS"
40 LET M = 5
50 PRINT "NUMBERS", "SQUARES", "PRØDUCTS"
60 PRINT
70 LET N(1) = N(2) = 1
80 LET S(1) = S(2) = 1
90 FØR I = 1 TØ M - 1
100 LET N(I + 2) = N(I + 1) + N(I)
```

```
110 LET S(I + 2) = N(I + 2)↑2
120 NEXT I
130 LET P(1) = 1
140 FØR I = 2 TØ M
150 LET P(I) = N(I − 1) *N(I + 1)
160 NEXT I
170 FØR I = 1 TØ M
180 PRINT N(I), S(I), P(I)
190 NEXT I
200 END


RUN


LIST ØF FIBØNACCI NUMBERS
```

NUMBERS	SQUARES	PRØDUCTS
1	1	1
1	1	2
2	4	3
3	9	10
5	25	24

GOODNESS-OF-FIT TEST

In statistical studies it is frequently necessary to determine whether the results of an experiment are significant or just due to random occurrence; the chi-square test is used for this purpose. For instance, the operators of a gambling casino may want to test all their dice for fairness and balance. Suppose each die is thrown 30 times and the observations are recorded in a frequency distribution showing the number of 1s, 2s, 3s, 4s, 5s, and 6s that came up. The frequencies of the outcomes are denoted, respectively, by $\emptyset_1, \emptyset_2, \emptyset_3, \emptyset_4, \emptyset_5$, and $\emptyset_6$. The theoretical frequencies, assuming the die is fair, are denoted by e_1, e_2, e_3, e_4, e_5, and e_6. From the actual and theoretical frequencies, a random variable u can be derived, where u is

$$u = \frac{(\emptyset_1 - e_1)^2}{e_1} + \frac{(\emptyset_2 - e_2)^2}{e_2} + \cdots + \frac{(\emptyset_6 - e_6)^2}{e_6}$$

The random variable u has a distribution closely approximated by the chi-square distribution with five degrees of freedom.

If the die is fair, each of the six outcomes can be expected to come up one-sixth of the time. Hence in 30 throws of the die, one may expect a theoretical frequency of five 1s, five 2s, and so forth. Suppose that the observed outcomes are the following:

1,2,6,5,3,1,1,5,6,3,1,3,4,5,3,3,6,2,1,4,2,3,5,2,5,2,1,6,3,6

A program written to calculate the value of u, for comparison with a tabulated value, is shown in Example 18. It is a general program to compute the fairness of any die or multi-sided gambling device with up to eight sides and with up to 30 observations.

Example 18

```
10 REM CHI SQUARE TEST PRØGRAM
15 DIM A(30),E(30),Ø(30)
20 LET N = 30' NUMBER ØF ØBSERVATIØNS
30 LET M = 6' NUMBER ØF SIDES TØ DEVICE
40 FØR I = 1 TØ N
50 READ A(I)
60 NEXT I
70 FØR I = 1 TØ M
80 LET E(I) = N/M
85 LET Ø(I) = 0
90 NEXT I
100 FØR I = 1 TØ N
110 IF A(I) = 1 THEN 170
120 IF A(I) = 2 THEN 170
130 IF A(I) = 3 THEN 170
140 IF A(I) = 4 THEN 170
150 IF A(I) = 5 THEN 170
155 IF A(I) = 6 THEN 170
160 IF A(I) = 7 THEN 170
165 IF A(I) = 8 THEN 170
170 LET K = A(I)
180 LET Ø(K) = Ø(K) + 1
190 NEXT I
195 LET U = 0
200 FØR I = 1 TØ M
210 LET U = U + (Ø(I) − E(I))↑2/E(I)
220 NEXT I
230 PRINT "VALUE ØF CØMPUTED CHI SQUARE IS", U
240 DATA 1,2,6,5,3,1,1,5,6,3,1,3,4,5,3
```

```
250 DATA 3,6,2,1,4,2,3,5,2,5,2,1,6,3,6
260 END
```

RUN

VALUE ØF CØMPUTED CHI SQUARE IS 2.8

The program in Example 18 first reads the values of N and M in lines 20 and 30. (If desired, an interactive INPUT statement could also have been used.) It then reads the 30 observed values at lines 40 to 60. At lines 70 to 90 the theoretical frequency is calculated. Lines 100 to 190 count the 30 observations and the frequency of each outcome. Lines 200 to 220 calculate the value of the chi-square random variable U, which is printed out at line 230. The calculated value can then be compared with tabulated values to determine if U is significant.

EXERCISES

1. Write a program which finds the sum of the series $n(n+1)/2$ for n $= 1, 2,..., 20$.

2. If a population of three million (not necessarily human) doubles every five years, how many years will it take to reach 300 million? Write a computer program to find out.

3. Write a program to compare the arithmetic mean and the geometric mean of the following set of data. Express the deviation in percent (plus or minus) from the arithmetic mean.

    66,8,55,14,14,41,39,74,53,42,34,99,66,48,15,20,73,60,44,34,45

4. Write a program to find the median of the following data:

    5,6,8,7,4,8,3,7

5. Write a program to find the mean and the standard deviation of the data in Exercise 4.

6. For a nine-horse race, you have been provided with relative weights giving each horse's chance of winning. The higher its weight, the better the horse's chances. The person who has given you the weights has little knowledge of probability theory, and

you are asked to change the weights into probabilities. Write a program to do so, given the weights listed below:

10,8,7,3,1,2,1,5,3

7. From past performance you know that the payoffs for winners are linearly related to the weights listed in Exercise 6. To be specific, a horse with a weight of 10 will pay $3, and a horse with a weight of 3 will pay $10. Write a program to calculate the expected payoff for each horse in the race.

8. Write a program to calculate the probability that, on a given day in a given maternity ward, if ten babies are born they will all be boys. Use the binomial distribution.

9. Write a program to make the same calculation as in Exercise 8, using the Poisson distribution and letting the average number of boys born on a given day be five.

10. Write an interactive program that will compute the batting averages of baseball players. Have the program print out the batting averages in decreasing order. The players' batting statistics are given below:

Player	Times at bat	Hits
Smith	109	29
Quade	102	33
Long	87	35
Small	113	26
Twang	101	39
Cook	128	42

11. Write a program to determine the chi-square variable u for the following experiment: The numbers formed by the first two digits of license plates on 50 randomly selected automobiles are to be tested as to whether they are actually random numbers between 00 and 99, inclusive. In your program, group the numbers in groups of ten (00 to 09, 10 to 19, etc.) and determine the frequency of each group. Theoretically each group should contain five data items if 50 observations are made.

18 MICROCOMPUTERS AND BASIC

MICROCOMPUTERS AND BASIC

Minicomputers or minis started as dedicated processors and controllers in the late 1960's. They are currently produced by a large number of manufacturers and are large enough to support multiple users, provide access to large files, and do a wide variety of business applications typically handled by large scale systems. Microcomputers or micros are a more recent development. Dubbed 'Computers on a Chip', they are competing with and supplanting minis in many applications. All the logic for the central processing unit (CPU) can be put on one or several silicon chips less than 1/4" square.

Microcomputers using BASIC are especially efficient for small business problem solving. Smaller businesses and doctor's and dentist's offices are especially proving to be fertile areas for adoption of microcomputer-based systems.

For use as a personal home computer numerous applications have been identified such as menu planning, personal finance, mathematics tutorial program, telephone directory, and a variety of games. As a small business computer it performs payroll calculations, keeps track of accounts receivable, accounts payable, cash journal, general ledger, inventory, and so forth.

Four examples of micros are shown in Appendix E. The Motorola M6800 and the IBM5110 are more expensive units but are supported by two firms with extensive computing experience. The Radio Shack (Tandy Corporation) TRS-80 and the Commodore International PET are low cost microcomputers that are affordable as home computers and sell for under $1000 in their simpler configurations. The four examples are selected because they provide reasonable local service if hardware problems develop. Although other microcomputers may be of higher quality and capability, service, if problems develop, may be difficult to obtain on a timely basis.

181

PROGRAMMING A MICROCOMPUTER

Microcomputers in the past have been characterized by rather simple instruction sets, because of limited storage space. For ease of operation most manufacturers of micros have adopted the BASIC language. Easily modified interpreters, along with ROM (Read-Only Memories), have made it possible to use an efficient high-level language such as BASIC. Most of the rules of BASIC that we have presented in this book are appropriate for microcomputers, despite some differences in commands and statements.

Before we can program extensively with micros, we need to understand the peculiarities of such systems. For one thing, there are two kinds of memory the user is concerned with internally. ROM (Read-Only Memory) stores the interpreter and determines to an extent what statements can be used. RAM (Random Access Memory) provides limited internal storage for programs and data. The size of RAM is limited for most micros. It can be expanded but usually at considerable additional cost.

Much of the programs, files and data must therefore be stored on auxiliary equipment, such as floppy disks, cartridge tapes or paper tapes.

Another typical characteristic of the microcomputer is the extensive use of systems commands, many of which are on easily manipulated switches. For example, note the simple program below processed on one of the smaller micros

```
      CLEAR       (A switch command to clear the screen)
      ENTER       (A switch to enter statements, similar to car-
                  riage return)
      READY
      10 INPUT S
      20 LET T = S*  .05 +S
      30 PRINT T
      RUN
      ?           (computer asks for a value)
      157.447     (answer)
      READY
```

USE OF SYSTEMS COMMANDS

As previously indicated, an increased number of commands are being utilized. For example, the TRS-80 provides a complete series of commands for editing, handling disk operations, and graphics. User programs are processed by the user, using such simple commands as LOAD, SAVE, EXIT, LIST, or RUN. For a more complete list of possible commands, refer to Special Commands Useful for Microcomputers in Appendix E.

STATEMENTS

Statements for microcomputers are for the most part modelled on those of larger computers. They include the normal Input-Output types (INPUT, READ-DATA, PRINT), the control types (FOR-NEXT, GOTO, GOSUB-RETURN, ON, IF, STOP, and END), the Assignment statement LET, and some special ones such as DIM and TAB.

The Motorola 6800 makes good use of RESTORE to reset data. This statement permits the first argument of the first data statement to be reassigned to the first variable of the next READ statement as illustrated below.

Example

```
READY
LIST
10 LINE = 80          (A command to specify the number of
                       characters that can be used in the line)
20 DATA 1,2,3
30 DATA 4,5,6
40 READ A,B,C,
50 RESTORE            (Resets buffer so that the program
                       output is the same as LET A = 1,
                       B = 2, C = 3, D = 1, E = 2, F = 3)
60 READ D,E,F
70 PRINT A,B,C,D,E,F
80 END
RUN
```

STRINGS AND CONCATENATION

A character string is a sequence of characters in a character expression. Some micros (IBM 5110) use a function (STR) to allow one to extract, combine, or replace specific characters in the string. To extract characters, for example, the following can be used:

```
10 A$= 'PRODUCTION REPORT'
20 STR(B$,1,10) = STR(A$,1,10)
```

In this case, line 20 extracts the first 10 characters for A$ and assigns them to the first 10 characters of B$. To combine characters, the following would be used:

```
10 A$= 'PRODUCTION'
20 B$= 'REPORT'
30 LET STR(A$,12,7) = B$
```

In this case, line 30 places the contents of B$ (REPORT) with the contents of A$ (PRODUCTION).

String concatenation on microcomputers is possible. By using special symbols (A$ or [ ] character) a series of string variables can be combined for printing. For example,

Example

```
110 A$ = "A"
120 B$ = "B"
130 C$ = "C"
140 D$ = A$ + B$ + C$ (or A$ [ ] B$ [ ] C$)
```

This would print

```
A B C all on one line
```

FUNCTIONS

Most systems support the functions detailed in Chapter 6, P. 53. Some systems also support RND which produces a set of uniformly distributed pseudo-random numbers. The LEN function is also very useful for providing a number of characters in a string variable specified by the function. Some systems also utilize the CHR$ function effectively to provide a single character string which is equivalent to the specified value. These functions are illustrated in the following Example

Example

```
100 PRINT INT ((B−A+1) * RND(O)−A)
110 LET A = LEN (Z$)
120 LET A$ = CHR$(63)
```

Functions developed by the user, using the DEF function can be utilized as described in Chapter 6.

FILE MANIPULATION

It is quite important to be able to handle Input-Output devices and files in microcomputer systems. A typical example to handle a disk would be:

Example

```
      BASIC, OF, NF
      RESIDENT BASIC 1.0
      READY
10 REM DEMO
20 PRINT "ENTER VALUE"
30 INPUT X
40 LET Y = (R*R) * 3.1416
50 PRINT "AREA OF CIRCLE WITH RADIUS"; R; "IS"; A
60 END
      RUN
```

This program is an example of taking OF (name of Old file the user wishes to load) and creating a new file (NF).

CHAINING

Some microcomputers are able to chain effectively, that is, end a program currently being executed, loading a new program, and begin executing the new program. For example,

```
60 A$ = "D80'
70 B$ = 'PROC 4'
80 CHAIN A$, B$
```

This partial program is designed to end a program now being executed on device D80 and chaining it to a procedure file called PROC 4.

For other specific microcomputer commands, statements, and special features, see the section on microcomputers in Appendix E.

ARRAY LIMITS

The BASIC used in many microcomputers is frequently more limited than that available on larger computer systems. For instance the Radio Shack TRS-80 used a version of BASIC that only allows single arrays instead of multiple arrays used on more extensive BASIC versions. The limitation of a single array is especially troublesome when BASIC programs written for other systems are to be used.

To respond to the above dilemma it is possible to convert a double array program to a single array program. Below is shown a program that needs to be converted.

```
10 DIM B (10, 6)
20 FOR I = 1 TO 10
30 FOR J = 1 TO 6
40 B(I, J) = 0
50 NEXT J
60 NEXT I
```

The converted program below stores the 60 (10 X 6) matrix entries into 60 vector entries.

```
100 DIM (106)
110 FOR I = 1 TO 10
120 FOR J = 1 TO 6
130 A (I * 10 + J) = 0
140 NEXT J
150 NEXT I
```

The matrix entries consists of (1,1), (1,2), (1,3), (1,4), (1,5), (1,6), (2,1), (2,2), . . . , (10,4), (10,5), (10,6). After transformation the vector entries consist of (11), (12), (13), (14), (15), (16), (21), (22), . . . , (104), (105), (106). Note that the digits that identify each entry are identical and in the same order for both the matrix and the vector.

This concludes the section on microcomputers. Each microcomputer has a sufficient number of unique features that can only be found in the respective micro's manual.

Appendix A: Vectors and Matrices

The BASIC computer programming language has been designed to facilitate operations on vectors and matrices. However, before one is able to use the BASIC vector or matrix operation features he must know something about them. It is therefore the intention of this appendix to provide a brief introduction to vectors and matrices and how they are or may be used.

VECTORS AND VECTOR OPERATIONS

A vector is essentially a list of variables or numbers, and a matrix is a tabular display of variables or numbers. As such, they are extremely useful in many areas outside of — as well as within — mathematics.

A vector may represent a point in space, or it may be used to represent quantities of several commodities. A scalar is a one-dimensional vector, a single constant such as 12 or a variable such as x.

Suppose that a manufacturing plant produces three products. The plant output can be represented by the three-dimensional row vector (x_1, x_2, x_3), or the three-dimensional column vector $\begin{pmatrix} x_1 \\ x_2 \\ x_3 \end{pmatrix}$. If output on a given day were 65, 75 and 90 units of the three products, respectively, the plant's output could be recorded by the three-dimensional row vector (65, 75, 90). Note that the order of the elements is important: the vector (90, 65, 75) is not the same as (65, 75, 90).

Vectors can be added together, subtracted from each other, and multiplied by each other provided they are of the same dimension. Also in vector multiplication the vector on the left must be a row vector and the vector on the right must be a column vector. Vector addition, subtraction and multiplication are illustrated in Example 1. Note that in vector addition or subtraction the corresponding elements are added, or subtracted from each other, and the result is another vector of the

187

same dimension. Vector multiplication, on the other hand, produces a scalar. The scalar is found by adding the products of the corresponding elements.

Example 1

$$\begin{pmatrix} 5 \\ 6 \\ 9 \end{pmatrix} + \begin{pmatrix} 4 \\ -3 \\ 2 \end{pmatrix} = \begin{pmatrix} 5+4 \\ 6-3 \\ 9+2 \end{pmatrix} = \begin{pmatrix} 9 \\ 3 \\ 11 \end{pmatrix}$$

$$\begin{pmatrix} 13 \\ 9 \\ 11 \end{pmatrix} - \begin{pmatrix} 6 \\ 10 \\ 4 \end{pmatrix} = \begin{pmatrix} 13-6 \\ 9-10 \\ 11-4 \end{pmatrix} = \begin{pmatrix} 7 \\ -1 \\ 7 \end{pmatrix}$$

$$(4,6,3) \begin{pmatrix} 3 \\ 1 \\ 2 \end{pmatrix} = 4 \cdot 3 + 6 \cdot 1 + 3 \cdot 2 = 24$$

Suppose we have the equation

$$a_1 x_1 + a_2 x_2 + a_3 x_3 + a_4 x_4 = b$$

which we would like to express in vector form. From the definition of vector multiplication we see that the equation

$$(a_1, a_2, a_3, a_4) \begin{pmatrix} x_1 \\ x_2 \\ x_3 \\ x_4 \end{pmatrix} = b$$

if multiplied out, would result in the original equation. If we let $a' = (a_1, a_2, a_3, a_4)$ and $x' = (x_1, x_2, x_3, x_4)$ then we can rewrite the equation as the vector equation

$$a'x = b$$

The primes on a and x indicate that they are row vectors; an unprimed symbol represents a column vector. Note that the vector variable x in the last equation is unprimed because it is a column vector; as such, it is identical to a non-vector variable. The context must always make clear which type of variable is being used. Sometimes vector variables are printed in boldface type for identification.

A vector may be multiplied by a scalar. To do this, we simply multiply each element of the vector by the scalar, as illustrated in Example 2.

Example 2

$$k(x_1, x_2, x_3) = (kx_1, kx_2, kx_3)$$

$$7(5, 3, 2) = (35, 21, 14)$$

$$4 \begin{pmatrix} a_1 \\ a_2 \\ a_3 \end{pmatrix} = \begin{pmatrix} 4a_1 \\ 4a_2 \\ 4a_3 \end{pmatrix}$$

MATRICES AND MATRIX OPERATIONS

Whereas a vector is a row or column of variables or constants, a matrix is several rows — or, if you like, several columns — of variables or constants. Matrices can be added or subtracted, provided that they are of the same size i.e., have the same number of rows and columns. Matrix multiplication is also possible, but the number of columns of the matrix on the left, the premultiplier, must equal the number of rows of the matrix on the right, the postmultiplier.

Capital letters are used to symbolize matrices, to differentiate them from vectors and variables. Technically a vector is a matrix with one row or one column. Thus, it is possible to multiply a vector and a matrix, provided they satisfy the constraint imposed above.

Matrix addition and subtraction are illustrated in Example 3. Note that they are simply extensions of the vector operations.

Example 3

$$A = \begin{bmatrix} 5 & 4 & 11 \\ 7 & 6 & 2 \\ 3 & 9 & 8 \end{bmatrix} \qquad B = \begin{bmatrix} 2 & 11 & 8 \\ 4 & 6 & 1 \\ 13 & 9 & 4 \end{bmatrix}$$

$$C = A+B = \begin{bmatrix} 5+2 & 4+11 & 11+8 \\ 7+4 & 6+6 & 2+1 \\ 3+13 & 9+9 & 8+4 \end{bmatrix} = \begin{bmatrix} 7 & 15 & 19 \\ 11 & 12 & 3 \\ 16 & 18 & 12 \end{bmatrix}$$

$$D = A-B = \begin{bmatrix} 5-2 & 4-11 & 11-8 \\ 7-4 & 6-6 & 2-1 \\ 3-13 & 9-9 & 8-4 \end{bmatrix} = \begin{bmatrix} 3 & -7 & 3 \\ 3 & 0 & 1 \\ -10 & 0 & 4 \end{bmatrix}$$

Example 4 illustrates matrix multiplication. Note that each row in matrix X is multiplied by each column of matrix Y, element by element. The sum of the products of each row-column multiplication then becomes an element of the resulting matrix Z. Also note that a multiplication of an $n_1 \times m_1$ matrix and an $n_2 \times m_2$ matrix results in an $n_1 \times m_2$ matrix, where n stands for the number of rows and m for the number of columns.

Example 4

$$X = \begin{bmatrix} 3 & 2 \\ 4 & 1 \\ 2 & 4 \end{bmatrix} \qquad Y = \begin{bmatrix} 2 & 3 & 4 \\ 5 & 1 & 2 \end{bmatrix}$$

$$Z = X \cdot Y = \begin{bmatrix} 3 \cdot 2 + 2 \cdot 5 & 3 \cdot 3 + 2 \cdot 1 & 3 \cdot 4 + 2 \cdot 2 \\ 4 \cdot 2 + 1 \cdot 5 & 4 \cdot 3 + 1 \cdot 1 & 4 \cdot 4 + 1 \cdot 2 \\ 2 \cdot 2 + 4 \cdot 5 & 2 \cdot 3 + 4 \cdot 1 & 2 \cdot 4 + 4 \cdot 2 \end{bmatrix} = \begin{bmatrix} 16 & 11 & 16 \\ 13 & 13 & 18 \\ 24 & 10 & 16 \end{bmatrix}$$

Example 5 illustrates multiplication of a vector by a matrix and multiplication of a matrix by a vector. Note that the results are vectors.

Example 5

$$x' = (5, 6, 2, 3, 4)$$

$$Y = \begin{bmatrix} 2 & 3 \\ 4 & 1 \\ 2 & 3 \\ 4 & 2 \\ 6 & 3 \end{bmatrix} \qquad Z = \begin{bmatrix} 3 & 4 & 2 & 6 & 1 \\ 4 & 1 & 5 & 2 & 7 \end{bmatrix}$$

$$y' = x'Y = (74, 45)$$

$$z' = Zx = \begin{pmatrix} 65 \\ 70 \end{pmatrix}$$

Matrices and vectors can be used to represent systems of several equations. For instance, the three equations in three unknowns

$$a_{11}x_1 + a_{12}x_2 + a_{13}x_3 = b_1$$

$$a_{21}x_1 + a_{22}x_2 + a_{23}x_3 = b_2$$

$$a_{31}x_1 + a_{32}x_2 + a_{33}x_3 = b_3$$

can be represented in vector-matrix format as

$$Ax = b$$

where

$$A = \begin{bmatrix} a_{11} & a_{12} & a_{13} \\ a_{21} & a_{22} & a_{23} \\ a_{31} & a_{32} & a_{33} \end{bmatrix} \qquad x = \begin{bmatrix} x_1 \\ x_2 \\ x_3 \end{bmatrix} \qquad \text{and} \qquad b = \begin{bmatrix} b_1 \\ b_2 \\ b_3 \end{bmatrix}$$

A square matrix is one with the same number of rows as columns. The inverse of a square matrix is a matrix which, if post-multiplied by the original matrix results in a third matrix that has ones along the diagonal and zeroes elsewhere. This resultant matrix is called an identity matrix and is represented by the capital letter I. For instance, the matrix I below is the 3×3 identity matrix:

$$I = \begin{bmatrix} 1 & 0 & 0 \\ 0 & 1 & 0 \\ 0 & 0 & 1 \end{bmatrix}$$

The inverse of the matrix A is symbolized by A^{-1}. Hence, from the above definition it follows that

$$I = A^{-1}A$$

Only square matrices have inverses.

If a vector is pre- or post-multiplied by an identity matrix the result is the same vector. That is,

$$Ix = x \qquad \text{and} \qquad x'I = x'$$

This is very important, because it provides us with a means of solving systems of equations, for instance the three simultaneous equations in three unknowns discussed above, which we represented with the vector-matrix equation

$$Ax = b$$

If we premultiply both sides of the equation by A^{-1} we obtain

$$A^{-1}Ax = A^{-1}b$$

which is equivalent to

$$Ix = A^{-1}b$$

or

$$x = A^{-1}b$$

Hence we have solved for the vector x whose elements are the three unknown x_i, by vector-matrix multiplication.

The unsolved problem, and also the more complicated one, is how to find the inverse of a square matrix. Fortunately, this can be accomplished in several steps. First we must be able to find the determinant D of a matrix. The determinant of a square matrix is a scalar quantity; for a 2 × 2 or a 3 × 3 matrix it is found as shown in Example 6. Note that the process consists essentially of adding the products of the elements on the forward diagonals and then subtracting the products of the elements on the backward diagonals. The evaluation of determinants of larger matrices gets rather complicated, and the reader should consult an introductory algebra text for the method. Note that the inverse of a matrix exists only if its determinant is not equal to zero.

Example 6

$$A = \begin{bmatrix} 3 & 2 \\ 6 & 7 \end{bmatrix} \quad B = \begin{bmatrix} 2 & 1 & 4 \\ 4 & 7 & 3 \\ 2 & 3 & 5 \end{bmatrix}$$

$$D_A = (3)(7) - (2)(6) = 9$$

$$D_B = (2)(7)(5) + (1)(3)(2) + (4)(4)(3) - (4)(7)(2) - (3)(3)(2) -$$

$$(5)(1)(4)$$

$$= 70 + 6 + 48 - 56 - 18 - 20$$

$$= 30$$

Next we must be able to find the transpose A' of a matrix A. The transpose is the matrix whose columns are the rows of the original matrix, and whose rows are the columns of the original matrix. Example 7 illustrates how a transpose of a matrix is formed.

Example 7

$$A = \begin{bmatrix} 5 & 6 & 7 \\ 3 & 2 & 11 \\ 14 & 7 & 9 \end{bmatrix} \qquad A' = \begin{bmatrix} 5 & 3 & 14 \\ 6 & 2 & 7 \\ 7 & 11 & 9 \end{bmatrix}$$

$$B = \begin{bmatrix} 4 & 5 & 9 & 11 \\ 6 & 3 & 2 & 1 \end{bmatrix} \qquad B' = \begin{bmatrix} 4 & 6 \\ 5 & 3 \\ 9 & 2 \\ 11 & 1 \end{bmatrix}$$

The cofactor of an element of a matrix is found by crossing out the row and column in which the element is located and then finding the determinant of the remainder of the matrix. The matrix of cofactors is the matrix formed by substituting the cofactor of each element into the original matrix and then adjusting signs as follows: If the sum of the row and column numbers of the element is odd, change the sign of the element; if the sum is even, leave the sign unchanged.

Now, finally, to find the inverse of a matrix A, we find the cofactor matrix of its transpose A' and divide each element by the determinant of A. Example 8 illustrates the complete process. Note that $\bar{A}^c$ is the cofactor matrix with unadjusted signs; in matrix A^c the signs have been adjusted.

Example 8

$$A = \begin{bmatrix} 5 & 6 & 4 \\ 3 & 7 & 1 \\ 2 & 2 & 4 \end{bmatrix} \qquad A' = \begin{bmatrix} 5 & 3 & 2 \\ 6 & 7 & 2 \\ 4 & 1 & 4 \end{bmatrix}$$

$$\bar{A}^c = \begin{bmatrix} 26 & 16 & -22 \\ 10 & 12 & -7 \\ -8 & -2 & 17 \end{bmatrix} \qquad A^c = \begin{bmatrix} 26 & -16 & -22 \\ -10 & 12 & 7 \\ -8 & 2 & 17 \end{bmatrix}$$

$$D_A = 38$$

$$A^{-1} = \frac{A^c}{D_A} = \begin{bmatrix} 13/19 & -8/19 & -11/19 \\ -5/19 & 6/19 & 7/38 \\ -4/19 & 1/19 & 17/38 \end{bmatrix}$$

AN APPLICATION

Suppose a department store with three branches sells products I, II, III and IV in the quantities shown below:

Branch	I	II	III	IV
1	5	3	4	9
2	6	2	7	6
3	4	4	8	4

(header: **Product** spanning I, II, III, IV)

The profit margins at the three stores are slightly different from each other and can be represented by the row vector $p' = (.50, .40, .45)$. The profit made on each product can be found by premultiplying the matrix of Sales S (the body of the table above) by the vector p'. Let the resultant vector be g'; the gross profits on the products are the elements of g' in order. The results are shown in Example 9, where the total gross profit $\bar{g}$ is the sum of the elements of g'.

Example 9

$$p' = (.50, .40, .45) \qquad S = \begin{bmatrix} 5 & 3 & 4 & 9 \\ 6 & 2 & 7 & 6 \\ 4 & 4 & 8 & 4 \end{bmatrix}$$

$$g' = p'S = (6.7, 4.1, 8.4, 8.7)$$

$$\bar{g} = 27.9$$

This example is, of course, relatively simple and small. However, a firm with several hundred products and numerous stores could utilize the technique to good advantage.

EXERCISES

1.   For the matrices

$$A = \begin{bmatrix} 4 & 5 & -6 \\ -3 & 4 & 1 \\ 2 & 3 & 2 \end{bmatrix} \quad B = \begin{bmatrix} 8 & 3 & 1 \\ 6 & -2 & 4 \\ 3 & 7 & -9 \end{bmatrix} \quad C = \begin{bmatrix} 4 & 9 & -3 \\ -2 & 7 & -8 \\ 5 & 3 & 1 \end{bmatrix}$$

show that

a. $(A + B) + C = A + (B + C)$
b. $AB \neq BA$
c. $A(B + C) = AB + AC$
d. $A(BC) \neq (AB)C$
e. $AI = A = IA$

2.   Determine the inverse of

$$A = \begin{bmatrix} 8 & 2 \\ 7 & 3 \end{bmatrix}$$

Appendix B: BASIC and Its Business Derivatives

Most advanced versions of BASIC are subsets of the original version developed at Dartmouth, and generally a program written in one version can run under the original version. The differences are generally in the additional capabilities and statements. Statements common to most versions are summarized in the following table.

Elementary Statements	Purpose
Arithmetic	
LET	Assigns numeric value to a variable
INPUT/OUTPUT	
INPUT	Processes data supplied while program runs
PRINT	Outputs data etc. on terminal printer
READ	Assigns values to variables from DATA statement
RESTORE	For recycling through complete set of DATA statements
Loop and Subroutine	
FOR	To cycle through a designated loop; begins loop
NEXT	Ends loop
GOSUB	To develop a subroutine
RETURN	Causes control to return to statement following original GOSUB statement
Logic (branch)	
GOTO	Unconditional transfer
IF–GOTO or IF–THEN	Conditional transfer

| STOP | Terminates program execution; can be more than one in program |
| END | Terminates program; last statement |

Documentation

| REM | Inserts a comment |

Commands

RUN or BEGIN	Executes program
NEW	Records new name for file
LIST	Enables printing to be performed
SAVE	Causes program currently in core to be saved under its file name

Matrix Functions

DIM	Defines maximum number of elements in matrix
READ or GET	Reads value of each element of matrix from DATA statement
ZERO	Sets elements of matrix to zero
CON	Sets all elements of matrix to 1
TRANSPOSE	For transposition and inversion of matrices
IDN	Sets up an identity
PRINT	Prints each element of a one- or two-dimensional matrix

ADD	
SUBTRACT	Use common BASIC symbols
MULTIPLY	
SCALAR MULTI-PLICATION	Multiplies each element of a matrix by a scalar value

Specification

| DATA | Supplies values to the READ statement |
| DIM | Assigns memory locations in an array or table (see Matrix Functions also) |

Special Statements Useful for Business

The following table records only a sampling of special keywords and statements useful for business applications. Typical versions have been chosen as follows (numbers refer to columns in the table):

1. BUSINESS BASIC (BASIC/FOUR Corporation)
2. BASIC (B1700 etc. – Burroughs)
3. EXBASIC (Control Data/ITS)
4. TIMESHARING BASIC (Data General)
5. BASIC-PLUS (Digital Equipment)
6. BASIC 1 (General Electric)
7. SYSTEM/3 BASIC (IBM)
8. BASIC-2 (NCR)

	1	2	3	4	5	6	7	8
Specification Statements								
CHANGE				X		X		
DIM – with strings	X	X	X	X	X	X	X	
RANDOMIZE/RANDOM				X				
I/O								
INPUT – LINE					X			
PRINT USING				X	X	X	X	
PRINT w/TAB	X	X	X	X	X	X		X
WRITE IMAGE			X					
Loop and Subroutine								
CALL				X		X	X	
FOR WHILE, FOR–UNTIL				X				
ON GOSUB				X				
Logic								
ON–GOTO or ON–THEN				X	X	X		X
ON ERROR–GOTO				X				
Utility								
CHAIN			X	X	X	X		X
TRACE ON						X	X	
TRACE OFF								X
WAIT					X			
System Commands*								
ASSIGN						X		
ATTACH						X		

*BASIC–PLUS uses the code NH (after RUN, LIST, etc.) to indicate that the header line is not typed. Hewlett-Packard 2000 etc. usually requires a hyphen in some of the above commands, such as DELETE. Exceptions are BYE and CATALOG. On the PDP-11, the user can depress a CONTROL/C key to terminate the listing of a program. Others require a BREAK key action.

	1	2	3	4	5	6	7	8
BYE/LOGOUT			X	X	X	X		X
CARD			X					
CAT/CATALOG				X				
CLEAR (on CALL/370)								
CLOCK			X		X			
COMPILE				X				
CONTINUE (CONT)				X				
DATE			X			X		
DEASSIGN				X				
DELETE			X	X	X	X	X	
DUMP			X	X				
HELLO/LOGON/LOGIN			X		X			
KEY				X				
LIST	X	X	X	X	X	X	X	X
LIST XX or LINE	X		X	X	X	X	X	X
NEW	X	X	X	X	X	X		X
OFF (on CALL/370)								
OLD	X	X	X	X	X	X		X
PRINT (calculator mode)			X	X	X			
PROCEED/RESUME				X				X
PUNCH				X				X
RENUMBER or RESEQUENCE	X	X	X	X		X	X	
REPLACE, REASSIGN, RENAME				X	X			
RUN	X		X	X	X	X	X	X
SAVE/UNSAVE	X		X	X	X	X	X	X
TAPE	X		X	X	X			X
TIME				X		X		X

Functions

	1	2	3	4	5	6	7	8
COM, CLG, LGT							X	X
COT							X	X
DEF	X	X	X	X	X	X	X	
INITIALIZATION (matrix)				X				
INPUT/INPUT V (matrix)	X	X		X	X		X	X
INV	X	X	X	X	X	X	X	X
LEN or SIZE				X	X			
NUM	X							
POS	X							
WRITE or PUT (matrix)			X	X	X		X	

File Commands

	1	2	3	4	5	6	7	8
APPEND								X
BACKSPACE						X		

	1	2	3	4	5	6	7	8
CATALOG				X	X		X	
IF END or END/FILE			X	X		X		
INPUT	X	X	X	X		X		
KILL, RUBOUT, PURGE					X	X	X	X
NAME–AS					X	X		
NEW				X	X	X	X	X
PRINT	X	X						X
OPEN/CLOSE	X		X		X		X	
READ, GET, LOAD			X	X	X	X	X	X
SAVE/UNSAVE/CLEAR					X	X	X	X
SCRATCH, DELETE, CLEAR						X	X	X

Editing and Documentation*

	1	2	3	4	5	6	7	8
DELETE	X							
EDIT	X							
MERGE	X							
REMARK (REM)	X	X	X	X	X	X	X	X

*The PDP–11 uses an exclamation mark for a COMMENT statement. For renumbering, General Electric BASIC uses a special editing command such as EDIT RESEQUENCE to change the lines in a program. The PDP–11 uses a special program to do this.

Appendix C: Additional BASIC Features Available for Some Systems

Functions*

Mathematical	FIX(X)	Returns the truncated value of X
	LEN(A$)	Finds string length
	PI	Retains a constant value of 3.1416
	RND(X)	Random numbers, range 0–1
System	DATE$(0%)	Returns the current date in the format 01–FEB–77
	TIME$(0%)	Returns the current time of day as a character string such as "05:30PM"

Logical Operators

Negation	NOT	Equivalence	EQV
Product	AND	Sum	OR
Implication	IMP	Exclusive	XOR

Additional Flowchart Symbols

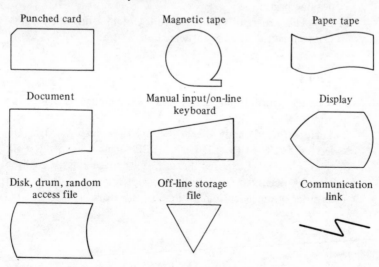

Punched card	Magnetic tape	Paper tape
Document	Manual input/on-line keyboard	Display
Disk, drum, random access file	Off-line storage file	Communication link

Features of the HIPO Template (See Figure C-1.)

1. Ease in drawing different-size boxes
2. Preprinted boxes for layout
3. Broad arrows to show transfers; narrow ones to show control flow
4. Off-page connectors
5. Cross-reference symbols
6. To symbolize large operations fully described on another diagram
7. Terminal symbol
8. To draw curves
9-11. Useful for text work

Summary of Debugging Techniques

Many errors that the beginning programmer makes are discovered by the BASIC compiler. These errors cause the printing of common diagnostic errors. Perhaps an equal number of errors, and far more difficult to locate, are caused by logic problems. Such errors may be found by running test data and noting that erroneous answers result — or that the computer does not respond properly. Some common techniques are these.

1. Desk check. Scan the program and any resulting output for obvious logic errors.
2. PRINT TRACE. Utilize a PRINT statement after each logical path or within each loop. Run test data and check results and heading printouts.
3. UTILITY programs (TRACE, etc.). Obtain a furnished utility from a manufacturer or software organization.

Types of Errors

1. Spelling errors, typing errors. May show a diagnostic message after typing.
2. Logic errors. Usually diagnostic messages such as OUT OF DATA or NO SUCH LINE NUMBER, or no diagnostic at all.
3. Syntax errors. Errors in the use of language rules. Usually a message occurs at the terminal, except for special errors such as order of precedence in arithmetic operators.

IBM

HIPO Template

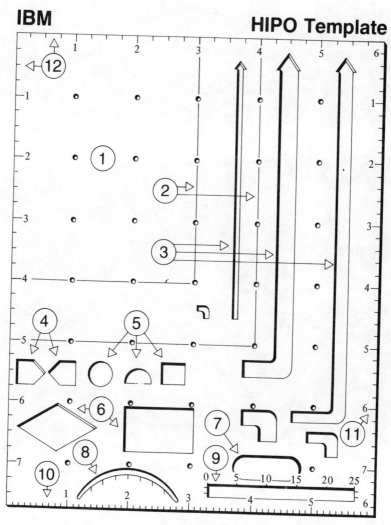

Figure C-1

Appendix D: Batch BASIC Summary and References

BATCH BASIC SUMMARY

Arithmetic Expression	**	for exponents
Rational Operators		
	.EQ.	Equal to
	.GT.	Greater than
	.GE.	Greater than or equal to
	.LT.	Less than
	.NE.	Not equal to
Logical Operators		
	.AND.	And
	.OR.	Or
	.NOT.	Not
PRINT		Use an apostrophe for quote
Statement Numbers (line numbers)		Optional, unless control is being transferred to a particular statement. If used, they must be in sequence.
DATA		On most systems, do not terminate with a comma

REFERENCES

Datapoint Corp. *Program User's Guide – DATAPOINT BASIC.* 1975.

De Rossi, C. J. *Learning BASIC Fast.* Reston, 1974.

Digital Equipment Corp. *BASIC-PLUS Language Manual.* 1975.

Edwards, P. and Broadwell, B. *Flowcharting & BASIC.* Harcourt, 1974.

Gershefsky, G. "Building a Corporate Financial Model." *Harvard Business Review*, July-August 1969, pp. 1-12.

Gottfried, B. S. *BASIC Programmer's Reference Guide*. Quantum, 1973.

Gruenberger, F. *Computing with the BASIC Language*. Canfield, 1969.

Hare, Van Court *BASIC Programming*. Harcourt, Brace & World, 1970.

Hirsch, S. *BASIC, A Programmed Text*. Melville, 1975.

Kemeny, J. G. and Kurtz, T. E. *BASIC Programming*. Wiley, 1971.

Appendix E: Commands and Statements of Four Selected Microcomputer Systems

Special Commands and Statements Useful for Microcomputers

	MOTOROLA M6800	IBM 5000	TRS-80 Level 11	PET
Special Commands	APPEND EXIT POKE TRACE-ON TRACE-OFF CONT CONTROL C,X,O PATCH LINE DIGITS	ALERT AUTO SKIP GO LINK MARK MERGE PROC RD RENUM UTIL	CLEAR CONT DELETE EDIT TROFF TRON	PEEK POKE SYS TI$ USR WAIT
Special Statements	RESTORE	CHAIN OPEN-CLOSE DELETE FORM GET PUT USE MAT PRINT USING	CMD ERROR ON ERROR GOTO OUT POKE RESET RESTORE RESUME SET PRINT USING	CLOSE GET LOAD OPEN POS RESTORE VERIFY SPC STEP

Appendix F: Solutions to Selected Exercises

CHAPTER 1

2. The computer requests a user number so that a record can be kept of the person using the computer via the teletypewriter terminal. If the computer is supplied by a commercial time-sharing organization, the user will be billed for the amount of time he used the computer (or at least part of the computer, since other users may use the computer simultaneously).

4. The terminal is best suited for processing relatively simple jobs that do not require large amounts of computer time. There are also more possibilities of errors by this method. Batch processing has been used for large amounts of data. New methods of input such as OCR may be of greater advantage.

6. Timesharing–Airline reservations, laboratory and hospital systems, military networks, pipeline companies, etc. Batch –Payroll processing, inventory control, market research data.

CHAPTER 2

2. a.   b.   c.

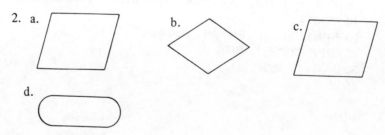

d.

CHAPTER 3

2.   There are 286 numeric variables in BASIC (excluding subscripted variables) because there are 26 letters in the alphabet, and each letter in the alphabet can be combined with one of the ten digits (0,1,2,3,4,5,6,7,8,9). Since letters by themselves are also numeric variables, there are a total of $26 \times 11 = 286$ numeric variables.

4. $5.6E10 = 56,000,000,000$; $.049E5 = 4900$; $46.2E-7 = .00000462$; $16.0E1 = 160$.

6.   a.   A/B C/D
      b.   10 DIM (50)
      c.   PRINT
      d.   E8
      e.   10 LET X = −3.5
      f.   **

CHAPTER 4

2.   10 LET B = 15.90
      20 LET A = 16.70
      30 LET A1 = (A + B)/2
      40 PRINT A1
      50 END

      RUN

      16.30

4.   5 REM THIS PRØGRAM PRINTS ØUT INVENTØRY LEVELS
      10 READ K,P
      20 PRINT "THE INVENTØRY LEVEL ØF ITEM"K
      25 PRINT "IS" P, "UNITS"
      30 DATA 12, 965
      40 END

      RUN

      THE INVENTØRY LEVEL ØF ITEM 12
      IS 965 UNITS

6. a.　10 LET Z = X/Y + 3
   b.　10 LET Z = (2* A * B/ (C+1) − T/(3* (P+T))) ↑ .33

8. 20 LET N1 = N

10. 50 PRINT C1,C2,C3

12. Not listed

14. 50:　　NAME　　AGE WEIGHT
    60: ########.####　###　##.##

CHAPTER 5

2. 10 REM THIS PRØGRAM LISTS ØUT NUMBERS
   15 REM 1 TØ 25
   20 FØR I = 1 TØ 25
   30 PRINT I;
   40 NEXT I
   50 END

   RUN

   1 2 3 4 5 6 7 8 9 10 11 12 13 14 15 16
   17 18 19 20 21 22 23 24 25

4. 5 REM THIS PRØGRAM CALCULATES THE AVERAGE
   10 REM ØF A SERIES ØF NUMBERS
   15 DIM B(20)
   20 FØR I = 1 TØ 14
   25 READ B(I)
   30 NEXT I
   40 LET S = 0
   50 FØR J = 1 TØ 14
   60 LET S = S + B(J)
   70 NEXT J
   80 LET A2 = S/14
   90 PRINT "THE AVERAGE IS" A2
   100 DATA −4, −3, −2, −1, 0, 1, 2, 3, 4, 5, 6, 7, 8, 9
   110 END

   RUN

THE AVERAGE IS 2.5

A simplified program consists of the following:

```
 5 REM THIS PRØGRAM CALCULATES AN AVERAGE
10 DIM B(20)
15 LET S = 0
20 FØR I = 1 TØ 14
30 READ B(I)
40 LET S = S + B(I)
50 NEXT I
60 LET A2 = S/14
70 PRINT "THE AVERAGE IS" A2
80 DATA −4, −3, −2, −1, 0, 1, 2, 3, 4, 5, 6, 7, 8, 9
90 END
```

RUN

THE AVERAGE IS 2.5

6.   The output for I, J, X, and Y is shown.

1	3	1	3
1	2	2	5
1	1	3	6
1	0	4	6
2	3	6	9
2	2	8	11
2	1	10	12
2	0	12	12
3	3	15	15
3	2	18	17
3	1	21	18
3	0	24	18

8.   Causes a condition to be tested, transferring according to whether
     the condition is true or false.

10.    ```
10 LET X = .07 * 2000
20 LET Y = .08 * 1800
30 IF X > Y THEN 60
40 PRINT "1" IS GREATER
```
```

```
50 GØ TØ 70
60 PRINT "2" IS GREATER
70 END
```

CHAPTER 6

2.
```
100 REM PRØGRAM TØ FIND MAXIMUM INTEGERS X
120 REM FØR WHICH Y=SQR(X) AND Y=EXP(X)
140 REM ARE LESS THAN 100
160 LET X = 0
180 LET X=X+1
200 LET Y = SQR(X)
220 IF Y < 100 THEN 180
230 PRINT "SQUARE RØØT"
240 GØ SUB 400
260 LET X = 0
280 LET X = X+1
300 LET Y = EXP(X)
330 IF Y < 100 THEN 280
350 PRINT "EXPØNENT"
360 GØ SUB 400
400 PRINT "THE LARGEST INTEGER FØR WHICH"
420 PRINT "Y < 100 IS" X-1
460 RETURN
500 END
```

```
RUN
```

```
SQUARE RØØT
THE LARGEST INTEGER FØR WHICH
Y < 100 IS 9999
EXPØNENT
THE LARGEST INTEGER FØR WHICH
Y < 100 IS 4
```

4. A value given to the function required in its operation. An example would be the (10) in INT (10).

6.
```
10 LET X = LØG (6.5 + 7.5)
20 PRINT X
30 END
```

8. a.   D**2; exponentiation
    b.   G**3; exponentiation
    c.   A * (D**2); multiplication
    d.   B * (G**3); multiplication
    e.   (B * (G**3))/C; division
    f.   (A * (D**2))+((B**3))/C); addition

CHAPTER 7

2. Not given.

4. You should select a name that reminds you of the program objective, according to the allowable length of the particular system.

6. We can check to see if our instructions have been carried out properly.

8. a.   Erases the working area and gives program a new name.
    b.   Erases program but not the name.
    c.   Erases working area and copies programs from both the storage and working areas.
    d.   Erases a program in storage area. (Was one of same name now in the working area.)
    e.   Replaces program in storage area with program of the same name now in the working area.

CHAPTER 8

2. Sets aside memory space for the array usage. It also gives the name and size of the memory space.

4.
```
10 DIM X (5)
20 FØR N = 1 TØ 5
30 READ X (N)
40 NEXT N
50 FØR K = 1 TØ 5
60 PRINT X (K)
70 NEXT K
80 DATA 8,42,21,25,20
90 END
```

6.
```
10 REM FINDS SMALLEST VALUE
20 DIM X (5)
30 FØR K = 1 TØ 5
40 READ X (K)
50 NEXT K
60 LET S = X (1)
70 FØR L = 2 TØ 10
80 IF S<X (L) THEN 100
90 LET S = X (L)
100 NEXT L
110 DATA 8,42,21,25,20
120 PRINT S
130 END
```

8. The output for the program is shown.

| 1561 | −60016 | .20822 | 64 | 3.333 |

CHAPTER 9

2.
```
100 DIM A(4,4), B(4,4), C(4,4)
110 MAT READ A
120 MAT B = INV(A)
130 LET S = DET
140 MAT C = A*B
150 MAT PRINT C;
160 DATA 1,2,3,2,1,2,3,2,1,2,3,2,1,2,3,2
170 END
```

RUN

1	0	0
0	1	0
0	0	1

4. Statement 10 is correct. Statement 20 is incorrect because only two matrices can be added in one statement; two statements should be used as follows:

```
20 MAT Y = Y + X
25 MAT Y = Y − B
```

Statement 30 is incorrect because the same matrix identifiers may not appear on both sides of the equal sign in a MAT multiplication statement. Statement 40 is correct. Statements 50 and 60 are incorrect because the same matrix identifiers may not appear on both sides of the equal sign in such statements. Statement 70 is correct; the same matrix identifier may appear on both sides of the equal sign in the case of addition.

6. To have close-packed matrices printed out, the matrix identifier following the PRINT statement must be followed by a semicolon.

8.  ```
    110 PRINT "LIST VECTØR ELEMENTS"
    120 MAT INPUT V
    130 LET N = NUM
    140 IF N = 0 THEN 300
    150 LET M = 10E−10
    160 FØR I = 1 TØ N
    170 IF V(I) > M THEN 190
    180 GØ TØ 200
    190 LET M = V(I)
    200 NEXT I
    210 PRINT "MAXIMUM ØF VECTØR ELEMENTS IS" M
    220 END
    ```

    ```
    RUN
    ```

    ```
    LIST VECTØR ELEMENTS
    ? 5,7,9,11,3,2,1,4
    MAXIMUM ØF VECTØR ELEMENTS IS 11
    ```

CHAPTER 10

2. The two kinds of variables used in BASIC are numeric variables such as A2, B0, C, D6, E3, F and G4, and string variables such as A$, B$, H$, P$, S$, and Z$.

4. `40 LET M$ = "FEB 1979"`

6. `10 INPUT X1,X2,X3,X$`
    ```

CHAPTER 11

2. Not given.

4. The following is a simplified program:

```
10 READ A,B,C,D
20 DATA 5,7,9,11
30 PRINT A + B − C, D/(A + B)
40 PRINT B↑A − C + D, A + B − C + D/(A + B) + 2
50 END

RUN

3          .916667
16809      5.91667
```

6.
```
100 REM WEIGHT TØ HEIGHT RATIØ PRØGRAM
105 PRINT "YØUR WEIGHT IN PØUNDS IS"
110 INPUT W
120 PRINT "YØUR HEIGHT IN INCHES IS"
130 INPUT H
140 LET R = W/H
150 IF R > 2.5 THEN 180
160 PRINT "YØUR WEIGHT IS SATISFACTØRY"
170 GØ TØ 200
180 PRINT "YØU ARE ØVERWEIGHT"
200 END

RUN

YØUR WEIGHT IN PØUNDS IS
? 160

YØUR HEIGHT IN INCHES IS
? 71

YØUR WEIGHT IS SATISFACTØRY
```

8.
```
100 PRINT "YØUR MØNTHLY SALARY IS"
110 INPUT S
```

```
120 PRINT "HØURS WØRKED PER WEEK ARE"
130 INPUT H
140 LET S8 = S/(H*4.33)
150 PRINT "YØUR HØURLY SALARY RATE IS $"S8
160 END
```

RUN

```
YØUR MØNTHLY SALARY IS
? 975
HØURS WØRKED PER WEEK ARE
? 36
YØUR HØURLY SALARY RATE IS $6.25
```

CHAPTER 12

2. The column order is sex, age, weight, height (inches), and last name.

100	MALE,	27,	165	71,	YØUNG
110	FEMALE,	45,	145,	68,	DAYNE
120	MALE,	23,	180,	73,	SMITH
130	MALE,	62,	175,	72,	FIELD
140	FEMALE,	37	155,	69,	JØNES
150	FEMALE,	52,	150,	70,	SMITH

4. No.

6.
```
100 FILES BILL
110 SCRATCH #1
120 END
```

8. The common-stock file will be named STK. The program below adds the latest closing price to the file.

```
100 FILES STK
110 DIM N$(20), Y(20), P(20)
120 LET N = 10
130 FØR I = 1 TØ N
140 READ #1, N$(I), Y(I)
150 READ P(I)
```

```
160 NEXT I
170 SCRATCH #1
180 FØR I = 1 TØ N
190 WRITE #1, N$(I), Y(I), P(I)
200 NEXT I
210 DATA 15.1, 16.4, 90.5, 47.9, 13.8
220 DATA 57.5, 125.5, 34.2, 25.4, 61.2
230 END
```

The resultant file will be listed out as follows if requested.

10 PAL,	15.4,	15.1
15 ADL,	16.3,	16.4
20 REN,	89.0,	90.5
30 PPQ,	47.8,	47.9
35 XØT,	13.9,	13.8
40 ZUN,	56.5,	57.5
50 FRT,	129.3,	125.5
55 BØV,	33.0,	34.2
60 FLT,	25.7,	25.4
70 GRT,	60.9,	61.2

10.
```
100 FILES BØND
110 DIM N$(60), C(60), Y(60), P(60)
120 PRINT "NUMBER ØF ENTRIES IN FILE"
130 INPUT N
140 PRINT "NAME", "CØUPØN", "YEAR", "PRICE", "R ØF R"
150 FØR I = 1 TØ N
160 READ #1, N$(I), C(I), Y(I), P(I)
170 LET R(I) = C(I)* 100/P(I)
180 PRINT N$(I), C(I), Y(I), P(I), R(I),
190 NEXT I
200 END
```

RUN

NUMBER ØF ENTRIES IN FILE
?3

NAME	CØUPØN	YEAR	PRICE	R ØF R
ADL	7.50	1979	89.50	8.38
PRQ	5.00	1992	63.50	7.87
DRK	8.75	1990	77.75	11.25

CHAPTER 13

2.   100 REM AFTER TAX RATE ØF RETURN
110 REM PRØGRAM FØR BØNDS
120 PRINT "BØND NAME, PRICE, CØUPØN AND TAX RATE"
130 INPUT B$, P, C, T' C AND T IN PERCENT
140 LET R = C*100/P*(1.00 − T/100)
150 REM R = RATE ØF RETURN AFTER TAXES
160 PRINT "AFTER TAX RATE ØF RETURN IS" R, "PERCENT"
170 END

RUN

BØND NAME, PRICE, CØUPØN AND TAX RATE
? RDR, 110, 12.1, 30
AFTER TAX RATE ØF RETURN IS 7.7 PERCENT

4.   100 REM PRESENT VALUE CALCULATØR
110 PRINT "TYPE PAYMENT, INTEREST RATE AND YEARS"
120 INPUT P, R, Y
130 LET V = P/(1 + R/100) ↑ Y
140 PRINT "PRESENT VALUE FØR PAYMENT ØF $" P
150 PRINT "AT INTEREST RATE ØF" R, "PERCENT"
160 PRINT "TØ BE MADE" Y, "YEARS HENCE"
170 PRINT "IS $" V
180 END

RUN

TYPE PAYMENT, INTEREST RATE AND YEARS
?1000, 10, 2
PRESENT VALUE FØR PAYMENT ØF $1000
AT INTEREST RATE ØF 10 PERCENT
TØ BE MADE 2 YEARS HENCE
IS $826.44

6.   The following program calculates the bonus each salesman will
receive on the basis of the first three months only.

100 REM BØNUS CALCULATIØN PRØGRAM
120 READ S,M' NUMBER ØF SALESMEN AND MØNTHS

```
130 DATA 6,3
140 FØR I = 1 TØ S
150 FØR J = 1 TØ M
160 READ B(I,J)
170 IF B(I,J) < =100 THEN 190
180 LET B(I,J) = 2*B(I,J)
190 NEXT J
200 NEXT I
205 LET T2 = 0
210 FØR I = 1 TØ S
220 LET T(I) = 0
230 FØR J = 1 TØ M
240 LET T(I) = T(I) + B(I,J)' TØTALS PØINTS
250 NEXT J
260 LET T2 = T2 + T(I)
270 NEXT I
280 PRINT "SALESMAN —— BØNUS DØLLARS"
290 FØR I = 1 TØ S
300 LET P(I) = T(I)/T2*20000
310 PRINT I, P(I)
315 NEXT I
320 DATA 53, 72, 121, 92, 91, 89, 60, 80, 122
325 DATA 59, 92, 60, 99, 97, 120, 95, 105, 109
330 END
```

RUN

SALESMAN — BØNUS DØLLARS

1	3350
2	2490
3	3500
4	1920
5	3980
6	4760

CHAPTER 14

2. The following program will find the economic order quantity and ordering lead time.

```
10 REM LEAD TIME AND EØQ PRØGRAM
```

```
20 LET N = 5' NUMBER ØF PARTS
30 FØR I = 1 TØ N
40 READ B(I), U(I), S(I), H(I), L(I)
50 REM BALANCE, USAGE, ØRDER CØST, HØLD CØST
55 REM LEAD TIME
60 LET B(I) = B(I) − U(I)
70 IF B(I) > U(I)*L(I) THEN 110
80 LET Q2 = 2*U(I)*S(I)/H(I)
90 LET Q(I) = SQR(Q2)
100 PRINT "FØR PART" I, "ØRDER" Q(I), "UNITS"
110 NEXT I·
120 DATA 1000, 160, 50, .0001, 5
130 DATA 3000, 570, 100, .0015, 4
140 DATA 25000, 1800, 40, .0075, 10
150 DATA 8000, 475, 10, .0005, 14
160 DATA 1475, 175, 50, .005, 8
170 END

RUN

FØR PART 5 ØRDER 1870 UNITS
```

CHAPTER 15

2.   200 LET X = 17*RND

4.   If three coins are tossed, the outcomes are 0, 1, 2, or 3 heads (or
      tails). The probabilities of the four possible outcomes are, respec-
      tively, 1/8, 3/8, 3/8, and 1/8.

```
100 REM PRØGRAM TØ SIMULATE THE
110 REM TØSSING ØF THREE CØINS
120 PRINT "NUMBER ØF TIMES CØINS ARE TØSSED"
130 INPUT N
140 LET S9 = 0
150 FØR I = 1 TØ N
160 LET R = RND
170 IF R < .125 THEN 260
180 IF R < .500 THEN 240
190 IF R < .875 THEN 220
200 LET H = 3
210 GØ TØ 270
```

```
220 LET H = 2
230 GØ TØ 270
240 LET H = 1
250 GØ TØ 270
260 LET H = 0
270 LET S9 = S9 + H
280 NEXT I
290 PRINT "NUMBER ØF HEADS ØN", N
300 PRINT "RANDØM TØSSES ØF THREE"
310 PRINT "CØINS IS" S9
320 END

RUN

NUMBER ØF TIMES CØINS ARE TØSSED? 10
NUMBER ØF HEADS ØN 10
RANDØM TØSSES ØF THREE
CØINS IS 17
```

6.
```
100 REM AUTØMØBILE SALES SIMULATIØN
110 READ N' NUMBER ØF DAYS
120 DATA 20
130 PRINT "AUTØMØBILE SALES"
140 LET T5 = 0
150 FØR I = 1 TØ N
160 LET X = INT(RND*10)
170 PRINT X,
180 LET T5 = T5 + X
190 NEXT I
200 PRINT "TØTAL SALES ØVER" N, "DAYS ARE" T5
210 END

RUN

AUTØMØBILE SALES
3      8      6      5      1
2      5      2      2      9
9      6      8      4      3
0      3      1      7      2
TØTAL SALES ØVER 20 DAYS ARE 86
```

8.
```
100 REM PØISSØN DISTRIBUTED AUTØ SALES
```

```
110 READ N,M' SIMULATED DAYS AND MAX SALES
120 DATA 20, 9
130 FØR J = 0 TØ M
140 READ X(J), P(J)
150 NEXT J
160 PRINT "AUTØ SALES"
170 LET T6 = 0
180 FØR I = 1 TØ N
190 LET Y = RND
200 FØR J = 0 TØ M
210 IF Y < P(J) THEN 230
220 NEXT J
230 PRINT X(J),
240 LET T6 = T6 + X(J)
250 NEXT I
260 PRINT "TØTAL SALES ØVER", N, "DAYS ARE" T6
270 DATA 0, .0498, 1, .1494, 2, .2240, 3, .2240
280 DATA 4, .1680, 5, .1008, 6, .0504, 7, .0216
290 DATA 8, .0081, 9, .0027
300 END

RUN

AUTØ SALES
1     2     1     3     4
3     1     6     2     3
0     3     3     1     7
2     4     0     4     3
TØTAL SALES ØVER 20 DAYS ARE 53
```

CHAPTER 17

2.
```
110 REM PØPULATIØN EXPLØSIØN PRØGRAM
115 REM P2 = INITIAL, M2 = FINAL PØPULATIØN
120 READ P2, 12, M2' 12 IS DØUBLING INCREMENT
130 DATA 3, 5, 300
140 LET Y2 = 0
150 LET P2 = P2*2
160 LET Y2 = Y2 + 12
170 IF P2 < 300 THEN 150
180 PRINT "PØPULATIØN WILL EXCEED" M2
190 PRINT "MILLIØN IN" Y2, "YEARS"
```

```
200 PRINT "ACTUAL PØPULATIØN IS" P2, "MILLIØN"
210 END

RUN

PØPULATIØN WILL EXCEED 300
MILLIØN IN 35 YEARS
ACTUAL PØPULATIØN IS 384 MILLIØN
```

4.
```
100 REM PRØGRAM FINDS MEDIAN
105 DIM D(100)
110 READ N' NUMBER ØF DATA ITEMS
120 DATA 8
130 FØR I = 1 TØ N
140 READ B(I)' VALUE ØF EACH DATA ITEM
150 NEXT I
160 DATA 5,6,8,7,4,8,3,7
170 REM RANKING SUBPRØGRAM
180 LET N1 = N2 = N − 1
190 FØR I = 1 TØ N1
200 FØR J = 1 TØ N2
210 IF D(J) < D(J + 1) THEN 250
220 D2 = D(J)
230 D(J) = D(J + 1)
240 D(J + 1) = D2
250 NEXT J
260 NEXT I
270 REM CHECK IF N IS EVEN ØR ØDD
280 LET H = N/2
290 IF H < INT(H) THEN 300
300 LET M = (D(H) + D(H) + D(H + 1))/2
310 GØ TØ 340
320 LET H = (N + 1)/2
330 LET M = D(H)
340 PRINT "THE MEDIAN IS" M
350 END

RUN

THE MEDIAN IS 6.5
```

6.
```
100 REM WEIGHTS TØ PRØBABILITY
```

```
110 REM CØNVERSIØN PRØGRAM
115 DIM W(50), P(50)
120 READ N
130 DATA 9
140 FØR I = 1 TØ N
150 READ W(I)' VALUES ØF WEIGHTS
160 NEXT I
170 DATA 10,8,7,3,1,2,1,5,3
180 LET S5 = 0
190 FØR I = 1 TØ N
200 LET S5 = S5 + W(I)' SUMS WEIGHTS
210 NEXT I
220 PRINT "THE PRØBABILITIES ARE:"
230 FØR I = 1 TØ N
240 LET P(I) = W(I)/S5
250 PRINT P(I),
260 NEXT I
270 END

RUN

THE PRØBABILITIES ARE:
```

.25	.20	.175	.075	.025
.05	.025	.125	.075	

8. Example 12 does not allow x or $N - x$ to be equal to zero. Note that the following program does allow it.

```
100 REM BIRTH PRØB. PRØGRAM—BINØMIAL
110 READ X,N,P
120 DATA 0,10,.50
130 IF X > 1 THEN 150
140 LET X = 1
150 LET S1 = 1
160 FØR I = 1 TØ X
170 LET S1 = S1*I
180 NEXT I
190 LET S2 = 1
200 FØR I = 1 TØ N
210 LET S2 = S2*I
220 NEXT I
```

```
230 IF N – X > = 1 THEN 250
240 LET N = N + 1
250 LET S3 = 1
260 FØR I = 1 TØ N – X
270 LET S3 = S3*I
280 NEXT I
290 LET B = S2/(S1*S3) * P ↑ X * (1–P) ↑ (N–X)
300 PRINT "PRØBABILITY ØF" X, "GIRLS IF" N
310 PRINT "BIRTHS ØCCUR IS" B
320 END

RUN

PRØBABILITY ØF 0 GIRLS IF 10
BIRTHS ØCCUR IS 9.77E–4
```

10.
```
100 REM BATTING AVERAGE CALCULATØR
105 DIM P$(25), T(25), H(25), A(25)
110 PRINT "HØW MANY PLAYERS";
120 INPUT N
130 PRINT "PLAYERS – TIMES AT BAT – HITS"
140 FØR I = 1 TØ N
150 PRINT "LIST";
160 INPUT P$(I), T(I), H(I)
170 NEXT I
175 PRINT "PLAYER – BATTING AVERAGE"
180 FØR I = 1 TØ N
190 LET A(I) = H(I)/T(I)
200 PRINT P$(I), A(I)
210 NEXT I
220 END

RUN

HØW MANY PLAYERS? 6
PLAYERS – TIMES AT BAT – HITS
LIST? SMITH,    109,    29
LIST? QUADE,    107,    33
LIST? LØNG,      87,    35
LIST? SMALL,    113,    26
LIST? TWANG,    101,    39
LIST? CØØK,     128,    42
```

```
PLAYER--BATTING AVERAGE
SMITH       .266
QUADE       .308
LØNG        .402
SMALL       .230
TWANG       .386
CØØK        .328
```

APPENDIX A

2. $A' = \begin{bmatrix} 8 & 7 \\ 2 & 3 \end{bmatrix}$ Det. $= (8)(3) - (7)(2) = 10$

$\bar{A}^c = \begin{bmatrix} 3 & 2 \\ 7 & 8 \end{bmatrix}$

$A^c = \begin{bmatrix} 3 & -2 \\ -7 & 8 \end{bmatrix}$

$A^{-1} \begin{bmatrix} .3 & -.2 \\ -.7 & .8 \end{bmatrix}$

INDEX

ABS function, 53
Absolute value, 53
Accounts, 153
Acoustic coupler, 3
Accumulators, subscript, 68
Alphabet, 13
Alter, 62
Arithmetic mean, 163
Arithmetic operations, 51, 52
Arithmetic operators, 18
Arithmetic series, 161
Array, 67, 71
Array, reverse order, 71
Array, variable, 67
Arrays, two dimensional, 72
Asterisk, 111
ASCII, 91
ATN function, 53
Average, 163, 164, 165, 172

Batch BASIC, 5
Batch processing, 5
Bayesian probabilities, 174
Binary file, 106
Binomial probabilities, 170
BCD, 106
Buffer, 115
Break-even analysis, 124
Branching, 35
BYE, 63

CALL statement, 199
CATALOG (CAT)a, 62
Central mean, 166
Central processing unit, 2
CHAIN statement, 115
Characters, 13
Character strings, 87
Chi-square, 177, 179
CLOCK command, 200
CLOSE statement, 115
Coding, 7
Comma, 25
Commands, 59
Comments, 17, 31
Compound interest, 126
Computed GO TO, 39
Computer, 2
Constants, 17, 22
Conversational language, 13
Cosine (COS), 53
Cost, 122
Cost behavior, 122

DAT$, 203
DATA statement, 22, 23
Debug, 7, 198
Decision table, 11
DEF statement, 55, 56
DELETE command, 62
Depreciation, 120

Desk check, 204
Deviations, 166
Device, 115
Digital Equipment Corp., vi, 3
DIM, 69
Documentation, 31

E Format, 18
Element, statement, 15
Elementary operations, 21
END statement, 31
Executable statements, 15
Execution, 1
EXP function, 53
Expected value, 168
Expression, 17

Fibonacci numbers, 176
FIELD statement, 115
File designation, 105, 108
FILE(S) statement, 105, 107
Financial model, 151
FIX(X), 203
Flowchart, 8
Flowchart symbols, 9
FOR-TO statement 42, 100
Functions, 52, 101

Geometric mean, 164
GET statement, 115
Goodness of fit, 177

GOSUB statement, 95
GO TO statement, 35

HELLO, 4
HIPO, 8, 204, 205
HIPO template, 205

IDN, 198
IF END#, 106
IF-THEN, IF GO TO, 40

Income statement, 157
INPUT#, 105
INPUT statement, 28, 137
INPUT-LINE statement, 92, 193
Input/output, 10, 22
INT function, 53, 55
Interactive, 28

Junior Merchant's problem, 145

Kemeny, J., 13
Keyword, 16, 21
KILL statement, 115
Kurtz, T., 13

Learning curve, 136
LEN(SV), 203
LET statement, 4, 21
Library, 110
Line numbers, 16
LIST command, 60
LOG function, 53
Logical errors, 7
Logical operators, 17
Loop, 36, 37, 42
Looping statements, 42, 43, 44
LSET word, 116

Machine language, 2
MAT, 76
MAT CON, 79
MAT IDN, 81
MAT INPUT, 84
MAT PRINT, 77
MAT READ, 77
Mathematical function, 53, 101
Matrices, vectors, 183
Matrix, 75
Matrix, multiple, 75
Matrix operations, 75
Matrix operators, 76, 79
Matrix transpose, 79

Median, 165
Message, 2
Minicomputers, 5, 181
Modes of operation, 2
Models, 151

National Science Foundation,
13
Nesting, 44
Nested loop, 44
NEXT statement, 42, 101
NEW statement, 60
Numbers, 17, 18, 21

Object program, 2
OLD command, 61
ON-ERROR GO TO, 199
ON GOSUB, 199
ON A GO TO, 38, 40
On-line, 2, 3
OPEN statement, 114
Order point, 131
Output control, 25

Password, 4
Payroll preparation, 119
Poisson probabilities, 172
Preliminary definition, 8
PRINT#, 106
PRINT statement, 25
PRINT TRACE, 204
PRINT USING, 27
PRINT WITH TAB, 199
Processing, 113
Production, 131
Program flowcharts, 8, 9
Programming, 14
Programming task, 1
PUT statement, 115

Queue, 146

RANDOM statement, 141
Random numbers, 141
Ratio scheduling, 133
READ statement, 22
READ#, 106
Relational symbols, 41, 90
REM, 17, 31
RENAME, 63
RENUMBER, 62
RESTORE, 105, 197
RETURN statement, 95
RND function, 203
RUBOUT, 200
RUN command, 3, 4, 29, 59,
198

SAVE command, 61
Scalar, 46, 169
Scalar multiplication, 192
SCRATCH, 105
Segment numbers, 8
Semicolon, 25
SGN function, 53
Simulation, 141, 143
SIN function, 53
Source program, 2
SQR function, 53, 54
Sort, array, 72
Statements, rules, 15
Statistical problem, 161
STEP expression, 100
STOP statement, 31, 38
Strings, 87, 89, 92
Structure, program, 14
Structured BASIC, 8
Subroutine, 95
Subroutine, independent, 98
Subroutine configuration, 95
Subscript, 67, 68
Subscripted variable, 67
Sum of a series, 161

Sum of the squares, 162
Symbolic name, 52
Symbology, 9, 13
System flowchart, 8
System commands, 59

TAB operator, 25, 26
Tangent function, 53
Teletype Corp., 3
Terminals, 1, 2, 3, 4
Testing, 7
TIME, 200, 203
TIME$, 203
Timesharing, 3
TRACE, 204
Transfers, 37
Transpose, 198

Truncated value, 39, 55

Unary minus, 18
UNSAVE command, 61
User, 5
Utility program, 204

Variables, 16, 17
Vector, 70, 181
Vector cofactor, 193
Vector statement, 85

WAIT statement, 199
WRITE#, 106

ZER, MAT, 81